The Ultimate Japanese Cookbook

111 Dishes From Japan To Cook Right Now

Slavka Bodic

Copyright @2021

All rights reserved. No part of this book may be reproduced in any form without writing permission in writing from the author. Reviewers may quote brief passages in reviews.

No part of this publication may be reproduced or transmitted in any form or by any means, mechanical or electronic, including photocopying or recording, or by any information storage and retrieval system, or transmitted by email without permission in writing from the publisher. While all attempts have been made to verify the information provided in this publication, neither the author nor the publisher assumes any responsibility for errors, omissions or contrary interpretations of the subject matter herein.

This book is for entertainment purposes only. The views expressed are those of the author alone and should not be taken as expert instruction or command. The reader is responsible for his or her actions. Adherence to all applicable laws and regulations, including international, federal, state and local governing professional licensing, business practices, advertising, and all other aspects of doing business in US, Canada or any other jurisdiction is the sole responsibility of the purchaser or reader.

Neither the author nor the publisher assumes any responsibility or liability whatsoever on the behalf of the purchaser or reader of these materials. Any perceived slight of any individual or organization is purely unintentional. Similarity with already published recipes is possible.

Imprint: Independently published

Please sign up for free Balkan and Mediterranean recipes:
www.balkanfood.org

Table Of Contents

INTRODUCTION 6
WHY JAPANESE CUISINE? 8
JAPANESE JOURNEY 10
BREAKFASTS 12
    Ochazuke 13
    Rice Sandwich (Onigirazu) 14
    Tamagoyaki Japanese Rolled Egg 15
    Japanese Rice Porridge (Ginger Honey Okayu) 16
    Dashi Eggs on Rice 17
    Japanese Garden Breakfast 19
    Okonomiyaki 20
    Japanese Omelet Rice (Omurice) 21
APPETIZERS AND SNACKS 23
    Pork Gyozas 24
    Prawn and Avocado Hand Rolls 25
    Japanese Rice Cakes (Onigiri) 26
    Karaage 27
    Sweet Chili Chicken Sushi 28
    Miso Eggplant with Pickled Vegetables 29
    Salmon and Avocado Rice Balls 30
    Takoyaki Octopus Balls 31
    Chestnut and Sweet Potato Mash (Kuri Kinton) 33
    Spicy Edamame 34
    Agedashi Tofu 35
SALADS 36
    Seafood Noodle Salad 37
    Octopus Salad (Tako Su) 38
    Shabu Pork Harusame Salad 39
    Daikon and Carrot Salad (Namasu) 40
    Seaweed Salad 41
    Candied Sardines (Tazukuri) 42
    Japanese Glass Noodle Salad (Harusame Salad) 43
    Broccolini Gomaae 45
    Shrimp and Broccoli Salad 46
    Japanese Potato Salad 48
    Spring Mix Salad with Miso Dressing 49
    Spicy Bean Sprout Salad 50
    Japanese Kani Salad 51
    Quinoa Prawn Sushi Bowl 52

SOUPS ... 53

- Tonkotsu Ramen Noodle Soup ... 54
- Kimchi and Tofu Soup ... 56
- Tamago Toji Udon Soup ... 57
- Butternut Squash Miso Soup ... 59
- Kabocha Pumpkin Potage ... 60
- Wonton Dumpling Soup ... 61
- Miso Broccoli Soup ... 63
- Ochazuke Chicken Rice Soup ... 64
- Kansai Ozoni Soup ... 65
- Creamy Salmon Miso Soup ... 66
- Miso Soup ... 67
- Japanese Ramen Noodle Soup ... 68
- Cheat's Chicken Ramen ... 70

MAIN DISHES ... 71

- Japanese Chicken Yakitori ... 72
- Miso Steak ... 73
- Smoked Salmon Avocado Sushi ... 74
- Japanese Katsudon ... 75
- Chuka-Fu Shredded Cabbage ... 76
- Tonkatsu Pork ... 77
- Seared Sirloin with Japanese Dips ... 78
- Spice-Crusted Tofu with Kumquat Radish Salad ... 80
- Japanese-Style Brown Rice ... 82
- Chicken Katsu Curry Burger ... 83
- Sushi Burrito ... 85
- Miso Caramel Chicken Wings ... 86
- Japanese Cream Stew ... 87
- Beef Mushroom Dashi Stew ... 89
- Curry Udon Noodles ... 91
- Unagi Don Grilled Eel Rice Bowl ... 92
- Cabbage Pork Nabe Hot Pot ... 93
- Tree Curry Rice ... 94
- Tofu and Salmon Gratin ... 95
- Hayashi Rice Stew ... 97
- Kimchi Nabe Hot Pot ... 98
- Yakisoba Fried Noodles ... 99
- Chaikin Tofu in Ginger Broth ... 100
- Kabocha Pumpkin Curry ... 102
- Shogayaki Ginger Pork ... 103
- Sukiyaki Hot Pot ... 104
- Horse Mackerel with Vegetables ... 105
- Mushroom Risotto with Grapefruit Duck Breast ... 106
- Chicken and Tomato Nimono Stew ... 108
- Lamb Loin with Mung Bean ... 109

Sesame Salmon with Coconut Rice	111
Oyster Gratin with Tofu Sauce	113
Miso Marinated Pork Roast	114
Matcha-Smoked Chicken	115
Sesame Chicken	117
Aubergine Miso Stir Fry	118
Miso Chicken Teriyaki	119
Taki Komi Rice Pilaf	120
Aubergine Somen Noodles	121

DESSERTS ... 122

Sakura Cherry Blossom Swiss Roll	123
Fluffy Japanese Pancakes	125
Ganache Filled Strawberry Daifuku	126
Strawberry Awayukikan Dessert	128
Strawberry and Red Bean Paste Dorayaki	129
Strawberry Amazake Pudding	130
Yuzu Matcha Truffles	132
Strawberry and Sweet Red Bean Mochi (Ichigo Daifuku)	133
Matcha Soy Milk And Azuki Pudding	134
Yuzu Cupcakes with Matcha Frosting	135
Gugelhupf Cake	137
Kashiwa Mochi	138
Mizu Manju with Azuki Bean Paste	139
Minazuki Rice Cake Topped With Azuki Beans	140
Japanese Kuri Youkan Chestnut Jelly Cake	141
Tricolored Hishi Mochi	142
Three Color Dango Dumplings	144

DRINKS ... 145

Calpis Japanese Drink	146
Japanese Slipper Cocktail	147
Japanese Cream Soda	148
Sakuranbo Bitter	149
Autumn Kaze	150
Kaoru Lavender Cocktail	151
Japan-no-cino	152
Hokkaido Ice	153
Niseko Sparkle	154

ONE LAST THING ... 161

Introduction

Do you want to celebrate the authentic Japanese flavors by cooking some delicious and native Japanese meals at home? Then you've reached the right place! This cookbook is going to introduce you to some of the most popular Japanese recipes and meals that you'll love. Whether they're from Southern or Northern Japan, the whole Island offers a unique culture and traditions of its own. History has left great influences on the culinary norms and cuisine of Japan. There are some geographical and climatic influences too; together, they make Japanese cuisine diverse in taste and form. So today, you'll going to discover all about the richness and diversity of this Asian food.

In particular, *The Ultimate Japanese Cookbook* will introduce to Japanese cuisine and its culinary culture in an engaging way that you must have never tried before. It brings you a wide variety of Japanese recipes in one place. This cookbook is great for all those who are always keen to cook healthy food and love to sample new and unique flavors. With the help of this Japanese cuisine cookbook, you can create a complete Japanese menu at home, or you can prepare all the special Japanese recipes on your special occasions and celebrations.

All in all, you will find popular Japanese meals and ones that you might not have heard of within this comprehensive cookbook. From nourishing rolled eggs in breakfast to all of the warming meat and noodles soups, the Japanese desserts, the drinks, the entrees, and healthy Japanese salads, etc., you can find them all. Plus, all these recipes are created in such a simple way that those who aren't familiar with the Japanese culture, food, and language can still try and cook them at home without facing much difficulty.

Japanese culinary culture and cuisine are indeed full of wonders. There's a great use of soy sauce, spices, vegetables, and meat. And, if you want to add all those healthy ingredients to your diet, then give this book a thorough read, and you'll uncover all your answers right away.

Here's what you'll find in this cookbook:

- Fun Facts about Japanese Cuisine
- Insights About Japan
- Breakfast recipes
- Side dishes and appetizers
- Main Dishes
- Japanese desserts
- Japanese Drinks

Let's try all these Japanese recipes and recreate a complete menu to celebrate the amazing Japanese flavors and aromas.

Why Japanese Cuisine?

My early memory of Japanese cuisine was of the Japanese mochi that I tried once when I was a teenager; ever since then, I knew that this cuisine must be full of flavorsome surprises to offer. Then a few years later, I started studying the cuisine in-depth and tried recreating a number of Japanese recipes at home. Japanese cuisine has no parallel, and you cannot mix it up with other Asian cuisines because it has a different mix of sauces and spices used to add a unique Japanese touch to every recipe. It's deeply influenced by Asian culinary cultures, and you can see that in the use of a variety of noodles and rice. And you'll also find great diversity in the application of different ingredients like the use of rice cakes, fish cakes, and hot pepper sauces, which are completely Japanese in origin. That's what I loved about this cuisine, its originality, and uniqueness.

Japanese people believe in eating healthy and nutritious food. So, you you'll explore a lot of nourishing food in this cookbook. There's extensive use of:

- Soybeans
- Soy sauce
- Pork, lamb, and beef
- Poultry and duck
- Sticky rice

It's actually the geography of Japan that has greatly influenced its cuisine and the meals. There's a prominent use of seafood, including all the fishes, oysters, and octopuses. Then you'll find meals like pork stews and poultry and hot seafood soups that are served with noodles and white rice. Serving dishes with white rice is a common culinary tradition: from sushi to pork and lamb curries, everything is enjoyed boiled rice. There are other recipes that you'll encounter on this flavorsome menu that mainly include:

- Chaikin Tofu in Ginger Broth
- Kabocha Pumpkin Curry
- Shogayaki Ginger Pork
- Shabu Pork Harusame Salad
- Sukiyaki Hot Pot
- Horse Mackerel with Vegetables
- Mushroom Risotto with Grapefruit Duck Breast
- Chicken and Tomato Nimono Stew

In desserts and beverages, there are several good options to choose from. The one that I like the most is the strawberry stuffed mochi that's so delightful in taste and mildly sweet due to its stuffing.

Japanese Journey

Japan is an interesting country to visit. It has a lot of cultural diversity to experience. People are super respectful, and there are so many places to explore in different parts of this Island. It's located in East Asia, the northwest part of the Pacific Ocean. Whatever information and the ideas of Japan we all have in our minds are often derived from the media, especially the movies, but when you actually visit the country and its different cities, the experience is completely different. Japan is bordered by the Sea of Japan on the western side and the Sea of Okhotsk on the North. Then there's the East China Sea and Taiwan on the South. It's surrounded by water. It's basically an archipelago consisting of 6853 islands in total. There are, however, five main islands that are named Hokkaido, Shikoku, Kyushu, Okinawa, and Honshu. Tokyo is one of the most visited cities of not only in Japan but also in the world. It's also the capitol the country, and other popular cities include Kyoto, Kobe, Osaka, Yokohama, Nagoya, Kukuoka, and Sapporo.

Like China and a few other Asian countries, Japan is also densely populated; it stands at eleven on the list of the world's most populated countries. It's highly urbanized, so you'll notice a lot of great infrastructure and amazing skyscrapers in urban centers of the country. However, a three fourth of the land is covered by mountainous terrain, so people mostly live in the coastal plains. Among the eight different regions of the country, it's the Greater Tokyo Area that's the most populous in the world, with a population of 37.4 million.

Due to its diverse geography, Japan has many interesting sites and landscapes to offer great experiences. If you really want to explore the country, then mark at least two weeks on the calendar for the visit because you'll need time you n to explore its untapped beauties. Japan has the 6th longest coastline in the world, which also provides access to its baby islands. Moreover, there are mountainous regions as well. Since the country is situated on the ring of fire, it's also the most hit region in the world when it comes to earthquakes, volcanic eruptions, and other natural disasters. There are 111 volcanoes in the country that are active; imagine the risks! This is the reason that most urban areas developed around the coastline. Japan is on the list as the country with the 17th highest natural disaster risks. But despite all the risks, the place is worth a visit! The Japanese culture, people, and their hospitality are quite amazing.

Contrast and complexity are some of the key features of this land; there are ancient cultures and traditions that still exist in some parts of the country. What I loved about this place is that people heavily focus on education. Great value is given to arts and aesthetics. Nara and Kyoto are the two cities that have beautiful gardens built. There are ancient temples and shrines that are built in different places, and I'd definitely recommend them.

Now that you're familiar with the country let's get started with some delicious Japanese meals.

Breakfasts

Ochazuke

Preparation time: 15 minutes
Cook time: 30 minutes
Nutrition facts (per serving): 271 cal (15g fat, 13g protein, 0g fiber)

This Japanese salmon rice mix is one healthy breakfast that can be served with bacon and radish salad on the side.

Ingredients (4 servings)
½ salmon fillet
1 pinch of salt
1 cup cooked Japanese rice
1 teaspoon Bubu arare (puffed rice pallets)
1 teaspoon shredded nori seaweed (kizami nori)
¼ teaspoon toasted white sesame seeds
2 sprigs mitsuba (Japanese parsley)
Wasabi, for taste

Ochazuke With Dashi
1 cup dashi (Japanese soup stock)
1 teaspoon mirin
1 teaspoon soy sauce
⅛ teaspoon salt

Preparation
At 425 degrees F, preheat your oven. Place the salmon on a baking sheet and bake it for 25 minutes until flaky. Season the salmon with salt and leave it for 10 minutes. Mix all the ingredients for Ochazuke in a saucepan and cook it to a boil. Add rice to a serving plate, place shredded salmon on top, and garnish with sesame seeds, nori, and rice crackers. Lastly, serve.

Rice Sandwich (Onigirazu)

Preparation time: 15 minutes
Cook time: 5 minutes
Nutrition facts (per serving): 248 cal (6g fat, 20g protein, 1g fiber)

Have you tried these egg mixed nori sandwiches for breakfast? Well, here's a Japanese delight that adds eggs, rice, and seaweed to your morning meal in a delicious way.

Ingredients (4 servings)
2 cooked rice bowls
2 Nori seaweed sheets
2 bacon slices
2 eggs fried, sliced
2 leaves lettuce

Preparation
Steam the seaweed in a saucepan filled with boiling water and then drain. Place the seaweed on a working surface and top them with cooked rice. Add the fried eggs, bacon, and lettuce leaves, and then roll the seaweed into a sandwich. Serve.

Tamagoyaki Japanese Rolled Egg

Preparation time: 15 minutes
Cook time: 10 minutes
Nutrition facts (per serving): 213 cal (8g fat, 19g protein, 7g fiber)

The Japanese Tamagoyaki rolled egg is famous for its delicious and warming flavors. Made from eggs, sugar, and salt, this egg roll goes well with all types of bread.

Ingredients (4 servings)
3 eggs
2 teaspoon sugar
½ teaspoon salt
2 tablespoon water
1 teaspoon olive oil

Preparation
Beat the eggs with sugar, salt, and water in a bowl. Add olive oil to a frying pan and heat over medium heat. Pour ⅓ of the egg mixture into the pan and cook until set. Roll the omelet from one side using a spatula, leaving ¼ portion to unroll. Next, push the roll to one side and pour ⅓ egg mixture. Cook until this layer is set. Fold the again and repeat the same steps with the remaining egg mixture. Transfer the egg roll to a plate and slice. Serve.

Japanese Rice Porridge (Ginger Honey Okayu)

Preparation time: 15 minutes
Cook time: 40 minutes
Nutrition facts (per serving): 270 cal (0.5g fat, 2g protein, 1.4g fiber)

Try this Japanese rice porridge for your breakfast, and you'll forget about the rest. The recipe is simple and gives you lots of nutrients in one place.

Ingredients (4 servings)
1 cup Japanese-style white rice
5 cups of water
1 tablespoon ginger, grated
1 teaspoon salt
4 tablespoon honey

Preparation
Add rice, ginger, and water to a cooking pot and leave for 30 minutes with the pot covered. Cook the mixture on medium-high heat first, and then reduce the heat to low and cook on low heat for 30 minutes. Remove the pot from the heat and leave it for 10 minutes. Garnish with honey and serve.

Dashi Eggs on Rice

Preparation time: 10 minutes
Cook time: 4 hours 20 minutes
Nutrition facts (per serving): 291 cal (3g fat, 13g protein, 2g fiber)

Dashi egg on rice is known as the classic Japanese breakfast, which is a good version of the basic rice and chicken mix. Plus, it's super and simple to make.

Ingredients (4 servings)
Dashi eggs
3 large eggs
¼ cup all-purpose chicken dashi
1 teaspoon caster sugar
¼ teaspoon salt
1 ½ cups cooked rice, hot
1 ½ tablespoon vegetable oil
2 tablespoon salmon flakes
2 teaspoon aonori (dried nori seaweed flakes)

Chicken dashi
1 lb. (500 g) chicken bones
About 3 liters of water
1 oz. (20 g) bonito flakes

Preparation
Beat the eggs with salt, sugar, and stock in a large bowl. Add oil to a pan and place it over medium heat. Pour the egg mixture into the pan and cook for a few seconds. Divide the omelct in half and flip to cook until set. Divide the rice into two serving bowls. Top the rice with one egg piece. Add salmon flakes and anoroi flakes. Prepare the dashi and add the chicken bones and enough water to cover them to a saucepan. Cook to a boil and then drain. Return the bones to a pan and add more water, then cover to cook for 4 hours on low heat. Add

bonitos' flakes and mix well. Allow the mixture to cool for 15 minutes, then strain. Serve the rice with the dashi. Enjoy.

Japanese Garden Breakfast

Preparation time: 15 minutes
Cook time: 15 minutes
Nutrition facts (per serving): 226 cal (2.4g fat, 14g protein, 1g fiber)

Here's one of the famous Japanese specialties, so everyone must try this interesting combination of soy dressing and veggies.

Ingredients (4 servings)
1 teaspoon rapeseed oil
1 garlic clove, grated
1 handful of kale, chopped
1 handful of spinach leaves
3 cherry tomatoes, quartered
3 shiitake mushrooms, sliced
3 regular mushrooms, sliced
4 eggs

Soy dressing
1 apple, grated
1 carrot, grated
1 onion, grated
½ cup (100 ml) soy sauce
½ cup (100 ml) rice vinegar
2 oz. honey

Preparation
Sauté the garlic with oil in a saucepan over medium heat until golden brown. Stir in the kale, spinach, mushrooms, and tomatoes. Sauté for 4-5 minutes, then make four wells. Crack one egg into each well and cover the lid. Cook for 4 minutes on low heat. Mix all the soy dressing ingredients in a bowl. Add this dressing on top of the eggs and garnish with chili. Serve.

Okonomiyaki

Preparation time: 15 minutes
Cook time: 6 minutes
Nutrition facts (per serving): 249 cal (11g fat, 14g protein, 0.7g fiber)

This Japanese okonomiyaki recipe is one good way to enjoy cabbage and green onion mixed pancakes in a savory style. Serve the freshly cooked pancakes with mayo sauce on top.

Ingredients (4 servings)
10 ½ oz. (300 g) flour
1 cup (220 ml) water
2 eggs
3 teaspoon baking powder
½ package dashi powder
¼ green cabbage, minced
4 spring onions, minced

Preparation
Mix flour with water, eggs, baking powder, and dashi powder in a bowl until smooth. Stir in the cabbage and spring onions and then mix again. Place a pan over medium heat and grease it with cooking spray. Add a spoonful of the batter and spread it into a round. Cook for 2-3 minutes per side until golden brown. Serve.

Japanese Omelet Rice (Omurice)

Preparation time: 15 minutes
Cook time: 4 minutes
Nutrition facts (per serving): 312 cal (8.4g fat, 12g protein, 1g fiber)

If you haven't tried the Japanese omelet rice before, then here comes a simple and easy to cook recipe that you can prepare at home in no time with minimum efforts.

Ingredients (2 servings)
½ onion, chopped
1 boneless, skinless chicken thighs, sliced
1 tablespoon olive oil
½ cup of frozen mixed vegetables
Salt, to taste
Black pepper, to taste
1½ cups cooked Japanese short-grain rice
1 tablespoon ketchup
1 teaspoon soy sauce

Omelet
2 large eggs
2 tablespoon milk
2 tablespoon olive oil
6 tablespoon sharp cheddar cheese

Preparation
Sauté the onion with oil in a pan until soft. Stir in the chicken and sauté until it changes its color. Toss in the mixed vegetables. Add black pepper and salt for seasoning. Add rice, soy sauce, and ketchup. Mix well. Beat 1 egg with 1 tablespoon milk in a bowl. Set a pan with 1 tablespoon olive oil over medium heat. Pour in the egg and cook for 1-2 minutes per side. Add cheese on top of

the eggs and fried rice. Press these layers, and then flip the pan over the plate. Garnish with ketchup. Serve.

Appetizers and Snacks

Pork Gyozas

Preparation time: 5 minutes
Cook time: 9 minutes
Nutrition facts (per serving): 158 cal (3g fat, 13g protein, 6g fiber)

Japanese pork gyozas are one of the most delicious appetizers to try. You can make different variations for its fillings and serve with different sauces.

Ingredients (12 servings)
5 oz. (150 g) minced pork
1 cup cabbage, shredded
2 green onions, chopped
1 teaspoon sesame oil
1 tablespoon soy sauce
1 inch piece fresh ginger, peeled, grated
2 garlic cloves, crushed
30 (275 g packet) gyoza wrappers
2 tablespoon vegetable oil

Dipping Sauce
2 tablespoon soy sauce
1 ½ tablespoon rice wine vinegar

Preparation
Mix the minced pork with garlic, ginger, soy sauce, sesame oil, green onion, and cabbage in a bowl. Place one wrap on the working surface and add 2 teaspoons of the minced mixture at the center of the wrap. Wet the edges of the wrapper and fold it to seal the filling. Pinch the edges to seal and repeat the same steps with the remaining wrappers and filling. Prepare and heat oil in a pan for frying and cook the gyozas for 2 minutes per side. Add ½ cup water to the pan and cover to cook for 5 minutes. Prepare the dipping sauce by mixing sauce and rice wine vinegar in a bowl. Serve the gyozas with the sauce. Enjoy.

Prawn and Avocado Hand Rolls

Preparation time: 15 minutes
Cook time: 22 minutes
Nutrition facts (per serving): 230 cal (4.2g fat, 10g protein, 1.4g fiber)

If you haven't tried the Japanese sensations before, then here comes a simple and easy to cook recipe that you can easily prepare and cook at home in no time with minimum efforts.

Ingredients (16 servings)
1 cup of sushi rice
¼ cup sushi seasoning
8 Obento nori sheets, quartered
2 teaspoon wasabi paste
1 large avocado, cut into strips
1 large yellow capsicum, cut into strips
32 cooked king prawns, peeled, deveined

Preparation
Rinse and drain the rice and add to a saucepan. Pour in 1 cup cold water and cover to cook. Boil, then reduce the heat to a simmer, and cook for 12 minutes until the water is absorbed. Remove from the heat and leave them for 10 minutes. Transfer the rice to a ceramic dish. Stir in the sushi seasoning and then mix well. Cut each nori sheet into four pieces. Place one nori sheet piece on the working surface and add a teaspoon of rice on top. Spread the rice in a layer and top them with wasabi, 1 prawn, 1 avocado slice, and 1 capsicum strip. Roll the nori shoot gently into a cone. Repeat the same with the remaining ingredients and nori sheet pieces. Serve.

Japanese Rice Cakes (Onigiri)

Preparation time: 15 minutes
Cook time: 18 minutes
Nutrition facts (per serving): 166 cal (3g fat, 3g protein, 0.1g fiber)

The appetizing rice cakes make a great addition to the menu, and they look great when served at the table.

Ingredients (4 servings)
2 cups short-grain rice
2 tablespoon soy sauce

Preparation
Rinse the rice under cold water and transfer them to a large saucepan. Pour in 3 ½ water and cover for 12-15 minutes on low heat. Remove the rice from the heat and leave them for 10 minutes. Fluff the rice with a fork, then take ¾ cup of rice packed firmly, and flip that rice cake over a plate. Repeat the same steps with the remaining rice. Shape the rice cakes into triangles and place them in a baking tray. Prepare and preheat a barbecue grill over high heat and cook the rice cake for 1 ½ minute per side. Brush the cakes with soy sauce as you grill them. Serve.

Karaage

Preparation time: 15 minutes
Cook time: 25 minutes
Nutrition facts (per serving): 381 cal (6g fat, 23g protein, 1g fiber)

If you haven't tried chicken Karaage before, then you must as these now as they have no parallel in taste and texture.

Ingredients (8 servings)
28 oz. (800 g) chicken thigh fillets, cut into 1-inch pieces
½ teaspoon salt
1 tablespoon sake (Japanese rice wine)
2 teaspoon mirin (sweet Japanese cooking wine)
2 tablespoon soy sauce
1-inch piece fresh ginger, grated
Vegetable oil, for deep frying
½ cup corn flour
Shredded green cabbage, to serve
Halved cherry tomatoes to serve

Preparation
Season the chicken with black pepper and salt in a bowl. Stir in the ginger, soy sauce, mirin and sake and then mix well to coat. Cover the chicken and marinate for 15 minutes. Remove the chicken from the marinade. Add oil to a saucepan and place it over medium-high heat. Dust the chicken with corn flour and sear them in the hot oil for 5 minutes per side until golden brown. Transfer the chicken to a plate using a slotted spoon. Serve with cabbage and tomatoes. Enjoy.

Sweet Chili Chicken Sushi

Preparation time: 10 minutes
Cook time: 32 minutes
Nutrition facts (per serving): 253 cal (1g fat, 24g protein, 0.2g fiber)

Who doesn't like to have chicken sushi every once in a while? Sushi lovers get ready to enjoy some heart-melting chicken and rice stuffed sushi on this menu.

Ingredients (6 servings)
1 cup of sushi rice
¼ cup Obento mirin seasoning
4 chicken tenderloins, cut into strips lengthways
¼ cup sweet chili sauce
2 teaspoon rice bran oil
2 tablespoon Kewpie mayonnaise
4 nori sheets
½ medium avocado, sliced
½ Lebanese cucumber, cut into strips
4 green oak lettuce leaves, torn

Preparation
Rinse the rice well and transfer to a saucepan. Pour in 1 cup cold water and cover to cook to a boil. Reduce the heat and cook for 12 minutes on a simmer. Remove the rice from the heat and leave them for 10 minutes. Transfer the rice to a ceramic dish and stir in seasoning. Mix well and allow the rice to cool. Stir the chicken with 2 tablespoon sweet chili sauce in a small bowl. Add the oil to a suitable pan and heat it over medium-high heat. Sear the chicken for 5 minutes per side. Mix the remaining sweet chili sauce and mayonnaise in a bowl. Place one nori sheet on a sushi mat. Add ¼ rice mixture and spread it. Add ¼ mayonnaise on top and place ¼ chicken, cucumber, avocado, and lettuce as well. Roll the nori sheet and repeat the same with the remaining ingredients. Serve.

Miso Eggplant with Pickled Vegetables

Preparation time: 15 minutes
Cook time: 2 hours 10 minutes
Nutrition facts (per serving): 201 cal (11g fat, 12g protein, 1g fiber)

Miso eggplant with pickled vegetables is one good meal to uplift your fiber intake. Try all the seasonings and sauces to enhance the taste.

Ingredients (4 servings)
¼ cup white miso paste
2 teaspoon soy sauce
2 garlic cloves, crushed
½ teaspoon sesame oil
2 tablespoon mirin seasoning
2 teaspoon caster sugar
2 eggplant, halved lengthways
1 cup of sushi rice
Pickled ginger, to serve
Green onion, sliced, to serve
Sesame seeds, toasted, to serve

Preparation
Mix 2 tablespoon water, sugar, mirin, oil, garlic, soy sauce, and miso paste in a bowl. Add 2 tablespoon of miso mixture to a slow cooker. Add the eggplants to the slow cooker and pour the remaining miso paste on top. Cover and cook for 2 hours on High heat with occasional stirring. Mix the cucumber, carrot, sugar, vinegar, 2 tablespoon water, black pepper, and salt in a bowl. Cover the veggies and leave them for 2 hours. Rinse the rice under cold water and cook as per the package's instruction. Drain the veggies and add to the eggplant. Serve with rice and garnish with green onion, ginger, and sesame seeds.

Salmon and Avocado Rice Balls

Preparation time: 15 minutes
Nutrition facts (per serving): 275 cal (9g fat, 16g protein, 2g fiber)

These salmon and avocado rice balls are another Japanese-inspired delight that you should definitely try. Serve with a flavorsome sauce.

Ingredients (6 servings)
2 cups of sushi rice, cooked
5 tablespoon sushi seasoning
½ small avocado, peeled, stone removed
½ small lemon, juiced
½ carrot, chopped
¼ Lebanese cucumber, chopped
1 ⅔ oz. (50 g) sliced smoked salmon, chopped
¾ cup sesame seeds, toasted
Soy sauce, to serve

Preparation
Mix the sushi rice with sushi seasoning in a bowl. Spread the rice on a baking sheet lined with parchment paper. Leave them for 1 hour. Mash the avocado flesh in a bowl and stir in lemon juice. Divide the rice into 16 equal portions and top each of them with 1 teaspoon avocado mixture. Add cucumber, carrots, and salmon on top of the rice. Roll the rice around the filling to make rice balls. Coat the balls with sesame seeds. Place these balls in a tray and cover to refrigerate for 1 hour. Serve fresh with soy sauce.

Takoyaki Octopus Balls

Preparation time: 10 minutes
Cook time: 4 minutes
Nutrition facts (per serving): 361 cal (13g fat, 15g protein, 1g fiber)

The Takoyaki octopus balls are another most popular snack in Japanese Cuisine, and they have this great taste from the flour batter and boiled octopus on the inside.

Ingredients (4 servings)
Batter
7 oz. (200 g) flour
2 eggs
2 cups (450 ml) water
Pinch of dashi stock powder

Fillings
3 ½ oz. (100 g) fresh boiled octopus, chopped
1 bunch spring onion, chopped
Red pickled ginger
Tempura flakes

Toppings
Takoyaki sauce
Japanese mayonnaise
Aosa powdered seaweed (or aonori)
Katsuobushi bonito flakes

Preparation
Beat 2 eggs with water, flour, and stock in a bowl until smooth. Place a Takoyaki plate over medium heat and grease its holes with cooking oil. Dice the octopus into pieces and add each piece into each hole of the plate. Pour the batter into

the holes. Top the batter with spring onion, ginger, and tempura flakes. Fry for 2 minutes, then flip the balls, and fry for 2 minutes. Thread balls on the skewers. Serve with Takoyaki sauce, mayonnaise, bonito flakes, and seaweed.

Chestnut and Sweet Potato Mash (Kuri Kinton)

Preparation time: 10 minutes
Cook time: 15 minutes
Nutrition facts (per serving): 274 cal (3g fat, 1g protein, 3g fiber)

What about a delicious chestnut and sweet potatoes mash? If you haven't tried it before, now is the time to cook this delicious mix at home using simple and healthy ingredients. Serve it with egg yolk on top as native Japanese do.

Ingredients (4 servings)
7 oz. (200 g) sweet potato
3 ½ oz. (100 g) candied chestnuts in syrup
2 teaspoon sugar

Preparation
Peel and cut the sweet potatoes into chunks. Add them to a saucepan and pour in enough water to cover them. Cook for 15 minutes, then drain. Mash the sweet potatoes in a bowl. Stir in half of the chestnuts and mash. Chop the remaining chestnuts and mix them with their syrup. Add this mixture to mashed potato and mix well. Serve.

Spicy Edamame

Preparation time: 10 minutes
Cook time: 7 minutes
Nutrition facts (per serving): 251 cal (7g fat, 8g protein, 6g fiber)

Spicy edamame is the best snack meal to find in Japanese cuisine. This mix is so loaded with crispy edamame with garlic and chili paste.

Ingredients (6 servings)
½ lb. edamame
1 tablespoon vegetable oil
2 garlic cloves, minced
2 teaspoon chili paste
1 tablespoon Miso Organic

Preparation
Prepare and boil the edamame as per the package instructions and transfer them to a boil. Sauté the garlic and chili paste with oil in a frying pan over medium heat until golden brown. Stir in the miso and cook for 1 minute. Toss in the edamame and then mix well. Serve.

Agedashi Tofu

Preparation time: 15 minutes
Cook time: 15 minutes
Nutrition facts (per serving): 249 cal (1g fat, 12g protein, 0.1g fiber)

The Agedashi tofu is everyone's favorite go-to meal when it comes to serving Japanese cuisine; you can prepare it in no time.

Ingredients (4 servings)
1 block medium-firm tofu
4 tablespoon potato starch
3 cups of vegetable oil

Sauce
1 cup dashi (Japanese soup stock)
2 tablespoon soy sauce
2 tablespoon mirin

Toppings
1 daikon radish, peeled and grated
1 green onion, chopped
Katsuobushi (dried bonito flakes)
Shichimi Togarashi, to taste

Preparation
Drain and squeeze the water from the tofu. Dice it into 8 pieces. Mix the mirin, soy sauce, and dashi in a small saucepan and cook to a boil. Then remove it from the heat. Coat the tofu with potato starch and deep fry them in hot oil until golden brown and crispy. Transfer the tofu to a bowl and pour the sauce on top. Garnish with radish, katsuobushi, green onion, and shichimi togarashi. Serve.

Salads

Seafood Noodle Salad

Preparation time: 15 minutes
Cook time: 10 minutes
Nutrition facts (per serving): 456 cal (15g fat, 16g protein, 0.7g fiber)

If you haven't tried this sensational salad, then here comes a simple and easy to cook recipe at home in no time with minimum efforts.

Ingredients (4 servings)
Salad
⅓ oz. (10 g) cooked prawns
⅓ oz. (10 g) smoked salmon, sliced
⅓ oz.(10 g) boiled octopus, sliced
5 lettuce leaves
1 serving ramen noodles

Dressing
1 teaspoon sesame oil
1 teaspoon soy sauce
1 teaspoon powdered dashi soup stock
½ teaspoon rice vinegar

Preparation
Boil the ramen noodles as per the package's instructions and then drain. Mix the soup stock with soy sauce, rice vinegar, sesame oil in a bowl. Mix the noodles, prawns, salmon, octopus, and lettuce leaves in a bowl and then pour the dressing on top. Toss well and serve.

Octopus Salad (Tako Su)

Preparation time: 10 minutes
Nutrition facts (per serving): 107 cal (8g fat, 23g protein, 1g fiber)

This salad makes a great side serving for the table, and you can use it with a range of delicious and healthy entrees.

Ingredients (4 servings)
¼ lb. octopus sashimi, sliced
⅓ English cucumber
½ tablespoon dried wakame seaweed
½ tablespoon toasted white sesame seeds

Vinaigrette
3 tablespoon rice vinegar
1½ tablespoon sugar
1 teaspoon soy sauce
⅛ teaspoon salt
1 teaspoon toasted white sesame seeds

Preparation
Soak the seaweed in warm water for 15 minutes and then drain. Mix the vinaigrette ingredients in a bowl. Toss in the sesame seeds, seaweed, octopus, and cucumber. Stir well and refrigerate for 30 minutes. Serve.

Shabu Pork Harusame Salad

Preparation time: 10 minutes
Cook time: 8 minutes
Nutrition facts (per serving): 589 cal (33g fat, 59g protein, 0.5g fiber)

This Japanese pork harusame salad makes a flavorsome mix of pork with harusame noodles; serve them for dinner or as a delicious lunch on your table.

Ingredients (4 servings)
10 ½ oz. (300 g) sliced pork
1 ⅔ oz. (50 g) harusame noodles
¼ onion, sliced
1 bunch watercress, sliced
4 lemon slices
2 teaspoons dried wakame seaweed
1 red chili

Dressing
1 tablespoon soy sauce
½ teaspoon salt
1 tablespoon sugar
½ teaspoon broad bean chili paste
2 tablespoon sesame oil

Preparation
Add pork and water to a saucepan, cook for 3 minutes, then add noodles. Cook until noodles are soft and then drain the mixture. Soak the wakame seaweed in a bowl filled with water for 5 minutes, then drain. Mix all the dressing ingredients in a bowl. Divide the pork and noodles in the serving bowls and top them with onion, lemon, watercress, red chili, and seaweed. Pour the dressing on top. Serve warm.

Daikon and Carrot Salad (Namasu)

Preparation time: 15 minutes
Nutrition facts (per serving): 266 cal (6g fat, 1g protein, 6g fiber)

Japanese daikon carrot salad is another nutritious yet simple meal for the breakfast table. It has lots of nutrients and fibers based on the combination of the veggies.

Ingredients (2 servings)
14 oz. daikon radish, peeled and julienned
3 oz. carrot, peeled and julienned
1 teaspoon salt
1 strip yuzu zest

Seasonings
1 ½ tablespoon sugar
1 ½ tablespoon rice vinegar
1 tablespoon water
¼ teaspoon salt

Preparation
Mix the sugar, rice vinegar, water, and salt in a salad bowl. Toss in the radish, carrot, and yuzu zest. Mix well and serve.

Seaweed Salad

Preparation time: 10 minutes
Cook time: 10 minutes
Nutrition facts (per serving): 127 cal (11g fat, 13g protein, 3g fiber)

It's as if the Japanese menu is incomplete without serving the classic seaweed salad. All you need is some seaweed, miso, and sauces, along with a sprinkle of sesame seeds, to debut this salad.

Ingredients (2 servings)
2 oz. of dried seaweed
1 tablespoon awase miso
1 tablespoon soy sauce
1 tablespoon mirin
1 tablespoon white roasted sesame seeds
1 tablespoon sesame oil
1 teaspoon rice vinegar
1 teaspoon yuzu juice
1 red chili, sliced
Pinch of sea salt

Preparation
Mix the seaweed with miso, soy sauce, mirin, sesame oil, sesame seeds, rice vinegar, yuzu juice, red chili, and salt in a bowl. Serve.

Candied Sardines (Tazukuri)

Preparation time: 10 minutes
Cook time: 5 minutes
Nutrition facts (per serving): 178 cal (16g fat, 4g protein, 2g fiber)

This candied sardine's meal tastes heavenly when cooked at home. Serve warm with your favorite toppings.

Ingredients (2 servings)
3 oz. (80 g) dried baby sardines
1 tablespoon mirin
2 teaspoon soy sauce
1 tablespoon toasted sesame seeds

Preparation
Toast the sardines in a cooking pan until golden brown. Next, add mirin, soy sauce, and sesame seeds. Sauté for 2 minutes and then serve warm.

Japanese Glass Noodle Salad (Harusame Salad)

Preparation time: 10 minutes
Cook time: 15 minutes
Nutrition facts (per serving): 213 cal (5g fat, 4g protein, 1g fiber)

The glass noodle salad is the right fit to serve with all your Japanese entrees. Here the harusame noodles are mixed with ham, cucumber, and carrot to make an amazing combination.

Ingredients (4 servings)
4 ¼ oz. Harusame (glass noodles)
2 tablespoons dried wakame seaweed
1 Japanese cucumber, peeled and julienned
⅓ carrot, peeled and julienned
½ teaspoon salt
3 black forest ham slices, julienned
2 teaspoon toasted white sesame seeds

Dressing
3 tablespoon rice vinegar
2 ½ tablespoon soy sauce
1 tablespoon sugar
1 tablespoon sesame oil (roasted)
1 tablespoon vegetable oil
Salt, to taste
Black pepper, to taste

Preparation
Rehydrate the harusame by boiling in water for 4 minutes, rinse under cold water, and drain. Slice the harusame to a bowl. Soak the wakame in water for 15 minutes and then drain. Transfer it to a harusame. Toss in the remaining salad

ingredients and mix well. Prepare the dressing by mixing their ingredients in a bowl. Pour the dressing over the salad and mix well. Serve.

Broccolini Gomaae

Preparation time: 10 minutes
Cook time: 4 minutes
Nutrition facts (per serving): 148 cal (1g fat, 13g protein, 1g fiber)

This broccolini salad is one delicious and healthy side meal, which has a refreshing taste due to the use of sugar, soy sauce, and sesame seeds in it. It's great to serve with skewers and meat dishes.

Ingredients (4 servings)
½ lb. broccolini ends trimmed
1 pinch salt
3 tablespoon toasted white sesame seeds
1 tablespoon soy sauce
1 tablespoon sugar

Preparation
Add water, a pinch of salt, and broccolini to a cooking pot and boil them for 2 minutes. Transfer the broccolini to an ice bath and drain. Transfer the broccolini to a bowl. Toast the sesame seeds in a frying pan for 1 ½ minute and then transfer to a mortar. Grind these seeds with a pestle. Stir in the soy sauce and sugar and then mix well. Add this sauce to the broccolini and mix well. Serve.

Shrimp and Broccoli Salad

Preparation time: 10 minutes
Cook time: 12 minutes
Nutrition facts (per serving): 261 cal (2g fat, 21g protein, 1g fiber)

The shrimp and broccoli salad are a refreshing side meal to serve with your entrees, and it is a must to serve with all the different entrees. Use this quick and simple recipe to prep in no time.

Ingredients (6 servings)
6 shrimp
½ tablespoon potato starch
1 pinch salt
1 tablespoon sake
6 oz. broccoli florets, boiled
1 avocado, peeled and diced
2 large eggs
1 Japanese cucumber, peeled and diced

Dressing
3 tablespoon Japanese mayonnaise
1 teaspoon milk
½ teaspoon salt
Black pepper, to taste

Preparation
Devein and clean the shrimp with starch. Add the shrimp to a pot filled with boiling water. Stir in the salt and the sake, and then cook for 2 minutes. Transfer the shrimp to a bowl place in ice-bath. Peel and dice the shrimp. Boil the eggs in water for 10 minutes, then transfer to an ice bath. Peel the eggs and dice them. Add the shrimp, eggs, cucumber, avocado, and broccoli to a bowl. Mix the

mayonnaise, milk, salt, and black pepper in a bowl. Add this dressing to the shrimp salad. Mix well and serve.

Japanese Potato Salad

Preparation time: 10 minutes
Nutrition facts (per serving): 351 cal (11g fat, 1g protein, 2g fiber)

As if the Japanese cuisine is incomplete without this potato salad. Made from boiled potatoes, carrots, cucumber, and some seasoning, these items offer lots of nutritional value.

Ingredients (4 servings)
2 boiled russet potatoes, peeled and diced
½ teaspoon salt
1 boiled egg, peeled and diced
2 ½ inch carrot, chopped
¼ cup of corn
2-inch English cucumber, peeled and chopped
2 slices black forest ham, diced
⅓ cup Japanese mayonnaise
Salt, to taste
Black pepper, to taste

Preparation
Toss all the potatoes, salt, egg, carrot, corn, cucumber, ham, mayonnaise, salt, and black pepper in a salad bowl. Serve.

Spring Mix Salad with Miso Dressing

Preparation time: 10 minutes
Nutrition facts (per serving): 145cal (2g fat, 11g protein, 1g fiber)

If you haven't tried the Japanese spring mix salad before, then here comes a simple and easy to cook recipe to serve today.

Ingredients (4 servings)
2 cups spring mix salad
1 avocado, sliced
1 red radish, sliced
3 mini heirloom tomatoes, sliced
4 mint leaves, torn
2 radish sprouts, discard the bottom

Sweet Miso Dressing
2 tablespoon M1nute Miso
2 tablespoon rice vinegar
1 tablespoon sesame oil (roasted)
1 tablespoon toasted white sesame seeds (ground)

Preparation
Whisk all the dressing ingredients in a salad bowl. Stir in the rest of the ingredients and toss well. Serve.

Spicy Bean Sprout Salad

Preparation time: 10 minutes
Cook time: 2 minutes
Nutrition facts (per serving): 300 cal (7g fat, 10g protein, 2g fiber)

This simple bean sprout salad is the first recipe that everyone should try on this menu. It is made out of lots of bean sprouts and a seasoning of Japanese seven spices.

Ingredients (4 servings)
12 oz. bean sprouts
1 tablespoon toasted white and black sesame seeds
2 tablespoon sesame oil (roasted)
1 ½ teaspoon soy sauce
1 ½ teaspoon Shichimi Togarashi (Japanese seven spice)
½ teaspoon salt
Black pepper, to taste
Green onion, chopped, for garnish

Preparation
Boil the bean sprouts in a pot filled with water for 2 minutes and then drain. Transfer the sprouts to a salad bowl. Stir in the rest of the ingredients and mix well. Serve.

Japanese Kani Salad

Preparation time: 15 minutes
Nutrition facts (per serving): 336 cal (17g fat, 27g protein, 1g fiber)

If you haven't tried the Kani salad before, then here comes something to make you say, "Arigato!"

Ingredients (4 servings)
5 oz. imitation crab meat (kanikama)
½ English cucumber, sliced
½ cup corn kernels

Ponzu Mayonnaise Dressing
2 tablespoon Japanese mayonnaise
1 tablespoon Ponzu
1 tablespoon toasted white sesame seeds
½ teaspoon soy sauce

Preparation
Shred the crab meat and transfer to a salad bowl. Stir in the cucumber and corn kernels, then mix well. Whisk the mayonnaise, ponzu, sesame seed, and soy sauce in a bowl. Add this dressing to the salad and mix well.

Quinoa Prawn Sushi Bowl

Preparation time: 15 minutes
Nutrition facts (per serving): 351 cal (10g fat, 22g protein, 6g fiber)

The Quinoa Prawn sushi bowl is a delight to serve at the dinner table. It's known for its comforting taste and its energizing combination of ingredients.

Ingredients (4 servings)
3 ½ oz. (100 g) white or brown sushi rice, boiled
1 oz. (20 g) mixed colored quinoa, boiled
1 ½ tablespoon rice wine vinegar
½ tablespoon golden caster sugar

Topping
1 teaspoon oil
½ sweet potato, sliced
8 large, peeled prawns, cooked
¼ cucumber, halved and sliced
½ avocado, sliced
1 roasted nori sheet, snipped
Sriracha mayonnaise and sesame seeds, to serve

Preparation
Toss all the quinoa ingredients in a salad bowl. Add the prepared topping.

Soups

Tonkotsu Ramen Noodle Soup

Preparation time: 15 minutes
Cook time: 14 minutes
Nutrition facts (per serving): 597 cal (46g fat, 31g protein, 4g fiber)

If you haven't tried the Tonkotsu noodle soup before, then you'll be totally surprised.

Ingredients (4 servings)
Soup
1 ½ cup (400 ml) Tonkotsu pork bone soup stock
½ tablespoon red miso
½ tablespoon Korean gochujang spicy miso paste
1 teaspoon lard
1 bunch ramen noodles

Pork mince
5 oz. (150 g) minced pork
1 tablespoon soy sauce
1 fresh red chili
1 garlic clove, minced
1 teaspoon vegetable oil
1 teaspoon sesame oil

Serve
Red pickled ginger
Nita Mago soy-marinated boiled eggs
Green onions, sliced
Nori seaweed sheets, cut in half

Preparation

Add the pork bone soup stock to a suitable saucepan and cook on a low simmer. Add the lard, miso paste, and red miso and mix well to combine. Keep this mixture on extremely low heat to keep it warm. Cook the ramen noodles as per the package's instruction and then drain. Sauté the pork mince with vegetable oil and sesame oil in a cooking pan until brown. Stir in the soy sauce, red chili, and garlic clove, then cook for 4 minutes. Divide the stock in the serving bowls, add noodles and sautéed pork. Garnish with ginger, eggs, green onions, and nori sheets. Serve.

Kimchi and Tofu Soup

Preparation time: 15 minutes
Cook time: 20 minutes
Nutrition facts (per serving): 417 cal (15g fat, 24g protein, 1.7g fiber)

A perfect mix of Kimchi with tofu is worth to try. Serve warm with your favorite side salad for the best taste.

Ingredients (4 servings)
1 ⅔ oz. (50 g) kimchi
½ pack tofu, diced
½ small onion, chopped
2 okra pods, destemmed
1 ½ teaspoon powder chicken stock
1 drops soy sauce
1 teaspoon ginger puree, optional
1 cup (200 ml) water

Preparation
Add the stock, soy sauce, and water to a saucepan and cook the mixture to a boil. Reduce its heat to medium. Add the onion, kimchi, and okra pods and cook for 5 minutes. Stir in the tofu cubes and cook for 10 minutes. Serve warm.

Tamago Toji Udon Soup

Preparation time: 10 minutes
Cook time: 20 minutes
Nutrition facts (per serving): 367 cal (6g fat, 19g protein, 1.2g fiber)

Try this soup with your family and make your meals special. I bet you'll never stop having it; that's how heavenly the combination tastes.

Ingredients (4 servings)
Udon noodles
10 ½ oz. (300 g) Udon flour
1 teaspoon sea salt
½ cup (130 ml) water
3 tablespoon Katakuriko potato starch for dusting

Tamago Toji egg drop soup
1 ½ cup (400 ml) dashi
1 tablespoon mirin
½ teaspoon sea salt
1 tablespoon soy sauce
2 eggs
1 tablespoon spring onions, chopped
Shichimi chili powder, to serve

Preparation
Mix the Udon flour, salt, and water in a bowl until it makes a smooth dough. Roll the dough with a rolling pin on a working surface. Fold and spread again 5 times. Cover the dough with cling film and leave it for 2 hours at room temperature. Transfer the dough to a floured working surface and spread it into 1cn thick sheet. Cut the dough into 1 wide strip. Boil the Udon noodles in a pot filled with boiling water for 10 minutes, then drain. Add dashi to a saucepan. Stir in the soy sauce, salt, and mirin and cook over medium heat, then boil. Beat

the egg in a bowl. Pour into the boiling soup and stir until the eggs turn into ribbons. Divide the soup into the soup bowls and garnish with spring onions and shichimi chili powder. Serve warm.

Butternut Squash Miso Soup

Preparation time: 15 minutes
Cook time: 20 minutes
Nutrition facts (per serving): 303 cal (14g fat, 8g protein, 1g fiber)

Japanese Butternut soup is always an easy way to add extra flavors and essential nutrients to your menu. So here's a gem to make in just a few minutes.

Ingredients (2 servings)
1 butternut squash, peeled and diced
1 onion, chopped
4 garlic cloves, minced
2 cups (500 ml) water
3 tablespoon unsalted butter
3 tablespoon white miso
1 tablespoon groundnut oil
1 pinch of salt
Black pepper, to taste
Fresh coriander
Sourdough bread, crusty, sliced

Preparation
Sauté the onions and garlic with half of the butter in a saucepan until golden brown. Toss in the butternut squash and sauté for 1 minute. Pour in the vegetable stock and cook for 15 minutes on a simmer. Mix 1 tablespoon miso with black pepper and the remaining butter in a bowl. Then add this mixture to the soup. Cook until the soup thickens and add black pepper and salt. Garnish with coriander and bread slices. Serve.

Kabocha Pumpkin Potage

Preparation time: 15 minutes
Cook time: 25 minutes
Nutrition facts (per serving): 365 cal (17g fat, 5g protein, 5.4g fiber)

It's about time to try some pumpkin potage on the menu and make it more diverse and flavorsome. Serve warm with your favorite herbs on top.

Ingredients (4 servings)
½ kabocha, Japanese pumpkin
½ onion, chopped
1 potato, sliced into rounds
1 oz. (30 g) butter
2 ½ cups (600 ml) vegetable stock
1 cup (200 ml) milk

Preparation
Sauté the onion with butter in a large saucepan for 5 minutes until caramelized. Peel the pumpkin and remove the seeds. Next, dice them into chunks. Add the pumpkin and potatoes to the pan and cook for 10 minutes. Stir in the stock and cook to a boil. Reduce the heat and cook on a simmer until the veggies are soft. Puree the mixture and add black pepper, salt, and milk. Mix well and garnish with parsley and croutons. Lastly, serve warm.

Wonton Dumpling Soup

Preparation time: 10 minutes
Cook time: 15 minutes
Nutrition facts (per serving): 323 cal (13g fat, 27g protein, 1.4g fiber)

Wonton Dumpling soup is here to make your meal special. You can always serve the mix with warm bread on the side.

Ingredients (4 servings)
Wonton
24 wonton wrappers
7 oz. (200 g) minced pork
2 teaspoon soy sauce
2 teaspoon cooking sake
⅔ oz. (25 g) leek, chopped
A pinch of pepper

Soup
1 garlic clove, chopped
2 tablespoon cooking sake
1 cup (200 ml) water
1 tablespoon chicken soup stock
1 tablespoon soy sauce
1 teaspoon salt
2 ½ tablespoon sesame oil

Vegetables
Leek, chopped
Carrot, chopped
Spinach, chopped
Shiitake mushrooms, chopped

Preparation

Mix 2 teaspoons of sake, a pinch of pepper, 2 teaspoon of soy sauce, meat, and leek in a bowl. Spread the wonton wraps on the working surface and then divide the filling at the center of the wrappers. Fold the wrappers to make wontons. Pinch the edges to seal the edges. Sauté the garlic with sesame oil in a saucepan until golden brown. Stir in 2 tablespoon of sake, boiling water, and 1 tablespoon soup stock. Mix and cook to a simmer. Stir in ½ tablespoon sesame oil, 1 tablespoon soy sauce, and 1 teaspoon salt. Add all the veggies and wontons; then cook for 5 minutes until soft.

Miso Broccoli Soup

Preparation time: 15 minutes
Cook time: 15 minutes
Nutrition facts (per serving): 253 cal (4g fat, 15g protein, 1g fiber)

The classic Japanese miso broccoli soup is here to complete your Japanese menu. This meal can be served on all special occasions and celebrations.

Ingredients (4 servings)
1 serving miso soup
4 broccoli florets
8 ½ oz. (240 g) quinoa
1 red chili, chopped
2 kale leaves, shredded
1 handful of alfalfa sprouts

Preparation
Boil and cook the quinoa as per the package's instructions. Place a steamer basket on top and add the broccoli. Then steam for 5 minutes. Prepare the miso soup in a saucepan as per the package's instructions. Stir in the quinoa, broccoli, kale, chili, kale, and alfalfa sprouts. Serve.

Ochazuke Chicken Rice Soup

Preparation time: 15 minutes
Cook time: 10 minutes
Nutrition facts (per serving): 522 cal (37g fat, 22g protein, 4g fiber)

Ochazuke with chilled chicken is an entrée that you must serve at the dinner table. This recipe will add a lot of flavors, aromas, and colors to your menu.

Ingredients (2 servings)
3 ½ oz. (100 g) cooked Japanese rice
½ cup (100 ml) ice water
1 tablespoon chicken stock
Chopped spring onion
Sweet pickles
Shredded nori seaweed

Preparation
Mix the chicken stock with water in a pan and warm it up over medium heat. Stir in the rice, spring onion, pickles, and nori seaweed. Serve warm.

Kansai Ozoni Soup

Preparation time: 15 minutes
Cook time: 35 minutes
Nutrition facts (per serving): 366 cal (21g fat, 1g protein, 1g fiber)

The Japanese Kansai Ozoni soup is here to complete your Japanese menu. This meal can be served on all special occasions and festive celebrations.

Ingredients (4 servings)
1 ½ oz. (40 g) daikon radish, sliced
1 carrot, sliced
2 taro potatoes, peeled and diced
1 ⅔ oz. (50 g) spinach, chopped
2 ⅔ oz. (80 g) white miso
2 mochi rice cakes
1 teaspoon katsuobushi bonito fish flakes
1 ½ cup (400 ml) water
1 small piece of kombu kelp
Yuzu peel to garnish

Preparation
Add the carrots and radish slices to a saucepan. Pour water to cover them. Boil the veggies for 9 minutes until soft, and then set them aside. Add the potatoes and cold water to a saucepan, cook for 9 minutes until soft, and then drain. Boil the spinach for 40 seconds and then rinse. Add the kombu kelp, fish flakes, and water to a saucepan. Cook the mixture for 10 minutes on a simmer and then strain this stock. Return the stock to a saucepan. Mix white miso with 1 ladle of stock in a bowl. Pour this mixture into the stock. Grill the mochi rice cakes for 2-3 minutes per side. Divide the mochi in the serving bowls. Add carrots, radish slices, potatoes, spinach, and miso soup. Serve warm.

Creamy Salmon Miso Soup

Preparation time: 10 minutes
Cook time: 35 minutes
Nutrition facts (per serving): 281 cal (16g fat, 19g protein, 2g fiber)

Salmon Miso soup is here to add flavors to your dinner table, but this time with a mix of broccoli and mushrooms. You can try it as an effortless soup bowl with some rice.

Ingredients (4 servings)
2 tablespoon white miso paste
1 sachet kombu dashi, mixed with 1 ½ cups water
1 tablespoon cooking sake
1 tablespoon mirin
1 ¼ cups (300 ml) soy milk
2 salmon fillets
1 pack shirataki noodles, drained
6 shiitake mushrooms, rehydrated
1 carrot
7 oz. (200 g) broccoli
1 potato

Preparation
Add the kombu dashi, water, miso paste, soy milk, mirin, and sake to a saucepan. Mix well and cook on low heat for 15 minutes. Add the veggies and cook until soft. Add the shirataki noodles and salmon. Finally, cook for 15 minutes. Serve warm with cooked rice. Enjoy.

Miso Soup

Preparation time: 15 minutes
Cook time: 7 minutes
Nutrition facts (per serving): 289 cal (4g fat, 17g protein, 1g fiber)

Miso soup is a must-have Japanese soup on this menu! Try a healing and nutritious combination of seaweed with tofu and dashi stock.

Ingredients (4 servings)
¼ oz. dried wakame seaweed
4 cups dashi stock
7 oz. (200 g) fresh silken tofu, cut into cubes
2 tablespoon white miso paste
3 tablespoon red miso paste
Spring onion, chopped, to serve

Preparation
Soak the wakame in a bowl filled with cold water for 5 minutes and then drain. Heat the dashi in a saucepan and stir in the tofu. Cook for 1 minute and then reduce the heat. Add the seaweeds and miso. Lastly, cook for 1 minute. Garnish with spring onions. Serve.

Japanese Ramen Noodle Soup

Preparation time: 15 minutes
Cook time: 20 minutes
Nutrition facts (per serving): 429 cal (12g fat, 51g protein, 6g fiber)

If you haven't tried the authentic Ramen Noodle soup before, then here comes a simple and easy to cook this recipe that you can recreate at home in no time with minimum efforts.

Ingredients (4 servings)
3 cups (700 ml) chicken stock
3 garlic cloves, halved
4 tablespoon soy sauce, plus extra to season
1 teaspoon Worcestershire sauce
1 thumb-sized piece of ginger, sliced
½ teaspoon Chinese five spices
1 pinch of chili powder
1 teaspoon white sugar
13 oz. (375 g) ramen noodles
⅔ lb. (400 g) sliced cooked pork or chicken breast
2 teaspoon sesame oil

Garnish
3 ½ oz. (100 g) baby spinach
4 tablespoon sweetcorn
4 boiled eggs, peeled and halved
1 sheet dried nori, finely shredded
Sliced green spring onions or shallots
Sprinkle of sesame seeds

Preparation

Mix the chicken stock with ginger, five-spice, water, chili powder, five-spice, Worcestershire sauce, soy sauce, and garlic cloves in a saucepan and then boil. Reduce the heat and cook for 5 minutes on a simmer. Stir in 1 teaspoon white sugar. Cook the ramen noodles as per the cooking instruction and drain. Slice the pork and sauté with 2 teaspoon sesame oil in a pan until golden brown. Divide the cooked noodles into four bowls and top them with meat, spinach, sweetcorn, and boiled halves. Strain the cooked stock and pour it into the four bowls. Garnish with spring onion, nori sheet, and sesame seeds. Serve.

Cheat's Chicken Ramen

Preparation time: 15 minutes
Cook time: 17 minutes
Nutrition facts (per serving): 255 cal (5g fat, 30g protein, 4g fiber)

You can give this chicken ramen a try because it has a good and delicious combination of chicken, bok choy, and mushrooms.

Ingredients (4 servings)
4 cups chicken stock
1 small pack of coriander, stalks, and leaves separated
1 red chili, sliced
2 tablespoon light soy sauce
3 ½ oz. (100 g) grey oyster mushrooms, sliced
3 ½ oz. (100 g) pack baby bok choy
2 cooked chicken breasts, sliced
3 ½ oz. (100 g) egg noodles
1 ⅔ oz. (50 g) sliced bamboo shoots

Preparation
Add the stock, coriander stalks, and chili to a large saucepan. Next, cook this mixture to a boil. Add water and then cook for 10 minutes on a simmer. Stir in the soy sauce, mushrooms, black pepper, chicken, noodles, and bok choy. Cook for 2 minutes. Divide the soup into the serving bowls and garnish with coriander leaves. Serve.

Main Dishes

Japanese Chicken Yakitori

Preparation time: 10 minutes
Cook time: 12 minutes
Nutrition facts (per serving): 262 cal (13g fat, 15g protein, 2g fiber)

If you can't think of anything to cook and make in a short time, then try this chicken yakitori recipe because it has great taste and texture to serve at the table.

Ingredients (6 servings)
½ cup soy sauce
¼ cup Massel chicken style liquid stock
¼ cup mirin
¼ cup caster sugar
2 lbs. chicken thigh fillets, trimmed, cut into 1-inch pieces
8 green onions, trimmed, cut into 1 ½ inch lengths
Steamed white rice to serve

Preparation
Mix the soy sauce, sugar, mirin, and stock in a small saucepan and place it over medium-high heat. Boil this mixture and cook for 5 minutes on medium heat until the sauce thickens. Thread the chicken and onions on the skewers alternately. Brush the prepared sauce over the skewers. Grill the skewers over medium-high heat for 6-8 minutes. Serve warm with rice.

Miso Steak

Preparation time: 10 minutes
Cook time: 6 minutes
Nutrition facts (per serving): 232 cal (9g fat, 32g protein, 0g fiber)

Try this miso-glazed steak with your favorite herbs on top. Adding a dollop of cream or yogurt will make it even richer in taste.

Ingredients (2 servings)
2 tablespoon brown miso paste
1 tablespoon dry sherry or the sake
1 tablespoon caster sugar
2 crushed garlic cloves
10 ½ oz. (300 g) lean steak
Baby spinach, sliced cucumber, radish, celery, and toasted sesame seeds, to serve

Preparation
Mix garlic with sugar, miso paste, and sherry in a Ziploc bag and add steak to the bag. Seal and shake the bag. Marinate the steak for 1 hour in the refrigerator. Prepare and preheat a grill over medium heat. Grill the steaks for 3 minutes per side. Serve with spinach, celery, cucumber, sesame seeds, and radish. Serve.

Smoked Salmon Avocado Sushi

Preparation time: 10 minutes
Cook time: 10 minutes
Nutrition facts (per serving): 369 cal (2g fat, 21g protein, 1g fiber)

Enjoy this classic avocado sushi with the twist of salmon. Serve this sushi with soy or chili sauce for great taste.

Ingredients (4 servings)
10 ½ oz. (300 g) sushi rice
2 tablespoon rice or white wine vinegar
1 teaspoon caster sugar
1 large avocado
Juice ½ lemon
4 sheets nori seaweed
4 large smoked salmon slices
1 bunch chives
Sweet soy sauce (kecap manis), to serve

Preparation
Boil the rice with 2 ½ cups (600 ml) water in a pot for 10 minutes. Next, stir in the sugar and vinegar. Cover and allow the rice to cool. Peel and slice the avocado flesh and transfer to a bowl. Add the lemon juice and mix well to coat. Spread the rice on the nori sheets and top with chives, salmon, and avocado. Roll the nori-sheets and serve. Slice the rolls into 8 pieces. Enjoy.

Japanese Katsudon

Preparation time: 10 minutes
Cook time: 13 minutes
Nutrition facts (per serving): 583 cal (21g fat, 34g protein, 4g fiber)

Make this Japanese Katsudon in no time and enjoy it with some garnish on top. Adding a drizzle of paprika also makes it super tasty.

Ingredients (4 servings)
1 teaspoon vegetable oil
1 large onion, sliced
1 breaded pork fillet, sliced
⅔ cup (150 ml) dashi stock
1 tablespoon soy
1 teaspoon mirin
1 teaspoon sugar
2 large eggs, beaten
7oz. (200 g) cooked rice
Chopped chives to serve

Preparation
Sauté the onion with oil in a pan until golden brown. Add the tonkatsu and top it with soy, dashi, sugar, and mirin. Beat the eggs and pour around the tonkatsu. Next, cook for 3 minutes. Serve warm with rice and garnish with chives. Enjoy.

Chuka-Fu Shredded Cabbage

Preparation time: 15 minutes
Cook time: 10 minutes
Nutrition facts (per serving): 103 cal (7g fat, 3 protein, 3g fiber)

Japanese chukka fu cabbage is also quite famous in the region; in fact, and it's a must to try because of its nutritional content.

Ingredients (2 servings)
½ green cabbage, shredded

Dressing
1 tablespoon white miso
1 tablespoon soy
1 tablespoon mirin
1 large lime, juiced
1 teaspoon sesame oil
2 tablespoon vegetable oil

Preparation
Toss the cabbage with miso, soy, mirin, lime juice, and sesame oil in a bowl. Sauté the cabbage mixture in a pan with the vegetable oil until golden brown. Serve.

Tonkatsu Pork

Preparation time: 10 minutes
Cook time: 10 minutes
Nutrition facts (per serving): 576 cal (25g fat, 42g protein, 2g fiber)

This tonkatsu is everything I was looking for to serve at my dinner table. Pork loin breaded with flour and breadcrumbs tastes heavenly when served with its special sauce.

Ingredients (4 servings)
4 thick boneless pork loin chops
3 ½ oz. (100 g) plain flour
2 eggs, beaten
3 ½ oz. (100 g) panko breadcrumbs
Vegetable oil, for shallow frying

Sauce
2 tablespoon ketchup
2 tablespoon Worcestershire sauce
1 tablespoon oyster sauce
2 teaspoon caster sugar

Preparation
Pound the pork loin in between a parchment paper with a mallet. Spread the flour on a plate, beat the eggs in a bowl, and add the breadcrumbs on a plate. Add the oil to a cooking pan and place it over medium heat. Coat the pork with flour, dip in the eggs and then coat with the breadcrumbs. Sear the pork chops for 5 minutes per side. Transfer the pork chops to a serving plate. Mix the Worcestershire sauce and sugar in a bowl. Serve the chops with the sauce.

Seared Sirloin with Japanese Dips

Preparation time: 15 minutes
Cook time: 12 minutes
Nutrition facts (per serving): 465 cal (28g fat, 46g protein, 1g fiber)

This Japanese sirloin meal is loved by all, young and adult. It's also simple and quick to make. This delight is great for dinner tables.

Ingredients (4 servings)
⅔ lb. (400 g) whole piece sirloin beef steak
1 tablespoon sunflower oil
1 thumb-sized piece ginger, grated
¼ cucumber, peeled and cut into matchsticks
Small handful mustard cress
2 teaspoon toasted sesame seeds
Cooked sticky rice to serve

Ponzu dipping sauce
4 tablespoon soy sauce
Juice 1 lime
Large pinch of chili flakes
1 small pinch of white sugar

Wasabi cream
1 tablespoon wasabi
5 tablespoon soured cream

Preparation
Mix the beef with the oil and seasoning in a frying pan and place it over medium heat and cook for 12 minutes for medium-rare, 10 minutes for rare, or 8 minutes for very rare. Meanwhile, prepare the ponzu sauce and mix all its ingredients in a bowl. Transfer the steaks to a plate and pour the sauce on top. Mix the sour

cream with wasabi in a bowl. Add the cream on top of the beef. Slice and garnish with sesame seeds and ginger. Serve warm.

Spice-Crusted Tofu with Kumquat Radish Salad

Preparation time: 5 minutes
Cook time: 20 minutes
Nutrition facts (per serving): 528 cal (33g fat, 27g protein, 12g fiber)

Try the Japanese crusted tofu with radish salad at the dinner, as the pork is breaded with a togarashi spice mix, along with flour and sesame seeds. In essence, you'll love it! Serve warm with your favorite sauces.

Ingredients (4 servings)
7 oz. (200 g) firm tofu
2 tablespoon sesame seeds
1 tablespoon Japanese shichimi togarashi spice mix
½ tablespoon corn flour
1 tablespoon sesame oil
1 tablespoon vegetable oil
7 oz. (200 g) tender stem broccoli
3 ½ oz. (100 g) sugar snap peas
4 radishes, sliced
2 spring onions, chopped
3 kumquats, sliced

Dressing
2 tablespoon soy sauce
2 tablespoon Yuzu juice
1 teaspoon golden caster sugar
1 small shallot, diced
1 teaspoon ginger, grated

Preparation
Cut the tofu in half and wrap them with kitchen paper to soak the excess water. Transfer the tofu to a plate and cut into slices. Mix the tofu with sesame seeds,

corn flour, and Japanese spice mix in a bowl. Mix the soy sauce, Yuzu juice, sugar, shallot, and ginger in a bowl. Boil water in a saucepan, add the vegetables, and cook until soft. Drain and strain the vegetables. Sear the tofu slices with cooking oil in a frying pan until golden brown. Divide the veggies in the serving bowls and pour the dressing on top. Toss well and top them with tofu. Serve.

Japanese-Style Brown Rice

Preparation time: 5 minutes
Cook time: 12 minutes
Nutrition facts (per serving): 308 cal (7g fat, 9g protein, 3g fiber)

This Japanese brown rice meal is a typical Japanese entree, which is a staple on the Japanese menu. It has this rich mix of rice with soybeans and soy sauce that I love.

Ingredients (4 servings)
5 ⅓ oz. (250 g) brown rice
6 oz. (175 g) frozen soya bean
1 tablespoon soy sauce
1 tablespoon olive oil
2 teaspoon ginger, grated
1 garlic clove, crushed
4 spring onions, sliced

Preparation
Boil the brown rice according to the cooking instructions. Add the soya beans and cook for 2 minutes. Mix the garlic, ginger, olive oil, and soy sauce in a bowl. Drain the rice mixture and transfer the mixture to a bowl. Pour the soy sauce mixture on top and garnish with spring onions. Serve.

Chicken Katsu Curry Burger

Preparation time: 5 minutes
Cook time: 12 minutes
Nutrition facts (per serving): 580 cal (18g fat, 50g protein, 8g fiber)

Simple and easy to make, this recipe is a must to try on this menu. Japanese chicken burger is a delight for the dinner table.

Ingredients (4 servings)
2 skinless chicken breasts
Vegetable oil for frying

Brine
2 cups (500 ml) milk
1 garlic clove, crushed
1 tablespoon shichimi togarashi

Katsu mayo
3 ¼ tablespoon (50 ml) ketchup
1 teaspoon toasted sesame oil
1 teaspoon soy sauce
1 tablespoon Worcestershire sauce
½ tablespoon runny honey
Juice from ½ lime
1 teaspoon hot mustard
2 teaspoon medium curry powder
3 tablespoon mayonnaise

Chicken katsu
1 egg
3 ½ oz. (100 g) rice flour
2 oz. (60 g) panko breadcrumbs

2 burger buns
1 handful iceberg lettuce, shredded
2 spring onions, sliced
2 radishes, sliced

Preparation

Mix the milk with garlic, shichimi, and 1 teaspoon salt in a bowl. Place the chicken in the brine, cover, and refrigerate for 3 hours. Mix all the ketchup with the sesame oil, soy sauce, Worcestershire sauce, honey, lime juice, hot mustard, curry powder, and mayonnaise in a bowl. Remove the chicken from the brine and place it in a tray. Beat the egg with 2 tablespoon brine in a bowl. Mix the panko with rice flour in another bowl. Dip the chicken in the egg mixture and coat with the panko mixture. Prepared and heat the oil in a deep-frying pan. Fry the chicken for 12 minutes and flip once cooked halfway through. Transfer the chicken to a plate and slice into 2-3 pieces. Cut the buns in half and toast them in a skillet. Add the chicken pieces, mayo, lettuce, onions, and radishes in between the buns. Serve.

Sushi Burrito

Preparation time: 5 minutes
Cook time: 25 minutes
Nutrition facts (per serving): 313 cal (11g fat, 18g protein, 4g fiber)

The Japanese sushi burrito is one of the traditional Japanese entrées and street food that's cherished around the world. It's made out of cucumber, carrot, tuna, and avocado filling.

Ingredients (4 servings)

5 oz. (150 g) sushi rice
2 teaspoon rice wine vinegar
½ cucumber, cut into matchsticks
1 carrot, cut into matchsticks
1 tablespoon soy sauce
4 nori sheets
2 teaspoon wasabi paste
1 ⅔ oz. (50 g) pickled ginger, chopped
1 lime, juiced
2 very ripe avocados, peeled and sliced
7 oz. (200 g) sushi-grade tuna steak, sliced
1 small pack coriander leaves, picked

Preparation

Rinse the rice and transfer to a saucepan. Cover the rice with water and cook for 10 minutes on medium heat. Leave the rice for 15 minutes. Add the vinegar and mix well. Allow the rice to cool. Toss the carrot with cucumber and soy in a bowl and marinate. Spread the nori-sheet on a sushi mat. Top them with the rice. Mix the wasabi with lime juice and ginger in a bowl. Top the rice with wasabi mixture, avocado, cucumber, tuna, and carrot. Roll the nori-sheet and slice. Serve.

Miso Caramel Chicken Wings

Preparation time: 5 minutes
Cook time: 55 minutes
Nutrition facts (per serving): 386 cal (22g fat, 24g protein, 1g fiber)

A perfect mix of chicken wings and miso caramel sauce is all that you need to expand your Japanese menu. Simple and easy to make, this recipe is a must to try.

Ingredients (6 servings)
2 tablespoon vegetable oil
4 tablespoon white miso
2 lbs chicken wings
3 ½ oz. (100 g) golden caster sugar
2 oz. (30 g) butter
½ lime, juiced
1 tablespoon sesame seeds

Preparation
At 375 degrees F, preheat your oven. Mix 2 tablespoon miso with oil and chicken wings in a large bowl. Spread the wings in a baking tray and bake for 45 minutes. Mix the sugar with 2 tablespoon water in a pan until dissolved and cook until the sugar is caramelized. Stir in the remaining miso and lime juice. Mix well and keep it aside. Pour the sauce over the chicken wings. Toss well to coat and garnish with sesame seeds. Bake again for 5 minutes and serve.

Japanese Cream Stew

Preparation time: 10 minutes
Cook time: 35 minutes
Nutrition facts (per serving): 301 cal (14g fat, 9g protein, 3g fiber)

Let's have a rich and delicious combination of cream stew with a rich taste. Try it with warm bread slices, and you'll simply love it.

Ingredients (4 servings)
2 tablespoon of vegetable oil
3 ½ oz. (100 g) of shiitake mushrooms
1 ⅔ oz. (50 g) of oyster mushrooms
1 white onion, sliced
2 potatoes, peeled, sliced, and cubed
3 carrots, peeled and sliced
½ broccoli, florets only
1 ½ cup (400 ml) of mushroom dashi

White sauce
1 oz. (30 g) of flour
2 tablespoons of butter
2 cups (450 ml) of milk
1 oz. (30 g) of cheese, grated

Koji
10 ½ oz. (300 g) of dried rice koji
Salt, to taste
2 cups (450 ml) of water

Preparation
Mix the rice koji with water and salt in a container. Then cover the lid and ferment for 3 days. Sauté the onions with oil in a large pan until soft. Stir in the

dashi and potatoes, and then cook to a boil. Reduce the heat to a simmer, then add carrots, and cook for 20 minutes on a simmer. Melt the butter in a saucepan, then stir in flour and cook for 2 minutes with occasional stirring. Pour in the cold milk and mix well until smooth. Cook for 5 minutes until the mixture thickens, and then stir in 3 ¼ tablespoon (50 ml) koji seasoning. Add this roux to the stew and then add the mushrooms and the broccoli. Cook the stew for 3 minutes. Stir in black pepper and salt. Serve warm.

Beef Mushroom Dashi Stew

Preparation time: 15 minutes
Cook time: 32 minutes
Nutrition facts (per serving): 496 cal (19g fat, 33g protein, 2g fiber)

This new version of beef mushroom dashi stew tastes amazing and is very simple and easy to cook. It's great for all beef and dashi lovers.

Ingredients (2 servings)
Stew
1 lb. (500 g) of beef tenderloin, cubed
⅔ lb. (400 g) of Japanese mushrooms, trimmed
1 tablespoon of coconut oil
5 ½ tablespoon (80 ml) of soy sauce
5 ½ tablespoon (80 ml) of mirin
2 teaspoon sugar
2 leeks, cut diagonally
1 ⅔ oz. (50 g) of watercress
3 tablespoon of shiitake mushroom powder

White rice
7 ½ oz. (210 g) of basmati rice
1 cup (200 ml) of water
1 cup (200 ml) of dashi, basic
Pinch of salt

Shiitake mushroom dashi
1 ½ oz. (40 g) of dried shiitake mushrooms
4 cups of water
Kombu, 1 postcard-sized piece

Preparation

Add the mushrooms, kombu, and cold water to a container, cover, and refrigerate for 8 hours. Strain the mushroom liquid and leave it aside. Sauté the beef with coconut oil in a cooking pan for 15 minutes. Mix the sugar, mirin, soy sauce, and shiitake powder in a bowl. Pour this mixture over the meat. Add 3 cups (710 ml) mushroom dashi and leeks. Cook this mixture for 40 minutes. Add the rice, remaining dashi, and water to a saucepan. Next, cook on low heat for 15 minutes. Stir in the mushrooms and cook for 2 minutes. Stir in the watercress and remove the stew from the heat. Serve warm.

Curry Udon Noodles

Preparation time: 15 minutes
Cook time: 30 minutes
Nutrition facts (per serving): 219 cal (13g fat, 8g protein, 3g fiber)

Here's a delicious and savory combination of Udon noodles, potato, and carrot that you must add to your menu.

Ingredients (4 servings)
2 blocks Japanese curry roux
½ onion, chopped
½ potato, chopped
½ carrot, chopped
2 packs pre-cooked Udon noodles
4 tablespoon tsuyu soup stock
2 ⅔ cups (640 ml) water
1 spring onion

Preparations
Add the onion, potato, carrot, and 1 cup (240 ml) water to a saucepan and cook for 20 minutes until soft. Add the curry roux and cook for 10 minutes with occasional stirring. Mix the soup stock and 1 ⅔ cups (400 ml) water in a pan and cook to a boil. Add the Udon noodles and cook until soft. Drain and transfer the noodles to the vegetable soup. Garnish with spring onions and serve warm.

Unagi Don Grilled Eel Rice Bowl

Preparation time: 15 minutes
Cook time: 18 minutes
Nutrition facts (per serving): 316 cal (7g fat, 24g protein, 12g fiber)

The Japanese unagi eel is famous for its juicy texture, unique taste, and aroma, so now you can bring those exotic flavors home by using this recipe.

Ingredients (2 servings)
2 ½ tablespoon sugar
1 ½ tablespoon cooking sake
4 tablespoon soy sauce
4 tablespoon mirin
7 oz. (200 g) rice
24 tablespoon (60 ml) water
2 eel fillets, skin-on

Preparation
Mix the sake with mirin in a saucepan and cook the mixture to a boil. Reduce its heat to medium. Add the sugar and mix until dissolved. Stir in the soy sauce and boil again. Cook for 10 minutes on a simmer. Then remove the mixture from the heat and allow it to cool. Strain the rice and add to a cooking pot, along with water to cook, until done. Meanwhile, preheat a grill at high heat. Cut the eel fillets in half and place them in a baking sheet, layered with aluminum foil. Brush the fillets with the oil and grill them for 7 minutes until golden brown. Brush the prepared sauce over the eel and grill again for 1 minute. Serve the eel and sauce over the rice. Enjoy.

Cabbage Pork Nabe Hot Pot

Preparation time: 15 minutes
Cook time: 15 minutes
Nutrition facts (per serving): 595 cal (10g fat, 39g protein, 3g fiber)

This cabbage Nabe hot pot is a must-have for every fancy dinner; thus, with the help of this recipe, you can cook them in no time.

Ingredients (2 servings)
½ Napa cabbage, chopped
⅔ lb. (400 g) pork, sliced
1 strip kombu kelp
4 tablespoon (60 ml) dashi stock
1 tablespoon light soy sauce
2 teaspoon soy sauce
1 tablespoon mirin
Yuzu peel
1 pinch of black pepper

Preparation
Add the dashi stock, soy sauce, mirin, and light soy sauce in a large pot and cook over medium heat. Stir in the kelp and pork and cook until the pork is done. Add the cabbage and cover the lid to cook until the cabbage is soft. Garnish with the yuzu peel and black pepper. Serve warm.

Tree Curry Rice

Preparation time: 15 minutes
Cook time: 30 minutes
Nutrition facts (per serving): 401 cal (7g fat, 9g protein, 2g fiber)

The refreshing Japanese curry always tastes great when you cook potato meat with onion, all together with spices and served with seaweed and rice.

Ingredients (6 servings)
Curry sauce
5 cubes Japanese curry mix
1 large onion, diced
1 large potato, diced
1 carrot, diced
3 ⅓ cups (800 ml) water

Serve
⅔ lb. (400 g) cooked Japanese rice
Aonori seaweed sprinkles or aosa powdered seaweed
White sesame seeds
Carrot and sweet potato slices cut into shapes

Preparation
Add water and vegetables to a cooking pot and cook for 20 minutes. Stir in the curry mix and mix well. Cook for 10 minutes on a simmer. Divide the soup in the serving bowl and add rice, seaweed, sesame seeds. Cut the carrots and sweet potato into decorative shapes using a cookie cutter. Add them on top of the curry rice. Serve warm.

Tofu and Salmon Gratin

Preparation time: 15 minutes
Cook time: 37 minutes
Nutrition facts (per serving): 289 cal (12g fat, 26g protein, 0g fiber)

Are you in a mood to have tofu with salmon on the menu? Well, you can serve this tofu and salmon gratin with a salad and rice.

Ingredients (4 servings)
5 oz. (150 g) firm tofu
3 ½ oz. (100 g) fresh spinach
10 ½ oz. (300 g) salmon fillets
½ leek
2 tablespoon flour
1 tablespoon butter
1 tablespoon vegetable oil
½ teaspoon miso paste
⅔ cup (150 ml) milk
½ teaspoon bonito stock granules
1 pinch of salt and black pepper
3 ½ oz. (100 g) aged cheddar
⅔ oz. (25 g) panko breadcrumbs
1 tablespoon parmesan

Preparation
Soak any excess liquid from the tofu block. Place the block in a bowl and heat it in the microwave for 1 ½ minute to release all excess water. Transfer the tofu to another bowl, and then mash it with a fork. Cook the spinach with water in a pan and then strain. Rub the salmon with black pepper and salt and then cut into cubes. Mix the salmon with spinach and leek in a bowl. Stir in flour and mix well. Melt butter in a pan and add vegetable oil. Toss in the salmon mixture and sauté until done. Stir in the milk, stock granules, tofu and miso, then mix

well and cook for 5 minutes until the mixture thickens. Spread this mixture in a casserole dish. Top the mixture with panko breadcrumbs and cheese and bake for 20-30 minutes in the oven. Serve warm.

Hayashi Rice Stew

Preparation time: 10 minutes
Cook time: 25 minutes
Nutrition facts (per serving): 492 cal (7g fat, 29g protein, 2g fiber)

Have you tried the Hayashi rice stew before? Well, now you can enjoy this unique and flavorsome combination by cooking this recipe at home.

Ingredients (4 servings)
7 oz. (200 g) beef, sliced
6 blocks Hayashi rice stew roux
1 teaspoon Worcestershire sauce
2 cups (500 ml) water
1 onion, chopped
1 carrot, chopped
3 ½ oz. (100 g) Asian mushrooms
2 tablespoon sesame oil
28 oz. (800 g) cooked Japanese rice

Preparation
Sauté the beef with sesame oil in a pan until brown. Next, pour in water, onion, mushrooms, and carrot and cook for 15 minutes on medium-low heat with occasional stirring. Add the roux and cook for 10 minutes and stir well. Stir in the Worcestershire sauce and mix well. Serve the stew with rice. Serve warm.

Kimchi Nabe Hot Pot

Preparation time: 15 minutes
Cook time: 20 minutes
Nutrition facts (per serving): 417 cal (8.1g fat, 13g protein, 0.6g fiber)

Japanese Kimchi Nabe hot pot is great to complete your menu, and this one, in particular, is great to have on a nutritious diet.

Ingredients (2 servings)
2 teaspoon kimchi base
⅔ cup (150 ml) tsuyu
1 packet tofu
3 ½ oz. (100 g) malony harusame noodles

Toppings
Shirataki noodles
Shiitake mushrooms
Carrot
Leek
Onion
Bean sprouts
Chinese cabbage
Spinach
Pork, beef, chicken
Prawns
Scallops

Preparation
Cook the noodles as per the package's instructions. Add the water, kimchi base, and tsuyu to a suitable pot. Next, boil the mixture. Add all the ingredients and mix well. Cook until the meat is cooked. Serve warm with the noodles.

Yakisoba Fried Noodles

Preparation time: 15 minutes
Cook time: 25 minutes
Nutrition facts (per serving): 347 cal (29g fat, 14g protein, 3g fiber)

Now you can quickly make flavorsome Japanese fried noodles at home and serve them to have a fancy meal for yourself and your guest.

Ingredients (4 servings)
1 portion yakisoba noodles
2 tablespoon yakisoba sauce
1 tablespoon mayonnaise
1 ⅔ oz. (50 g) pork, sliced
½ onion, chopped
⅛ white cabbage, chopped
¼ green pepper, chopped
1 small carrot, chopped
Aonori powdered seaweed
Pickled shredded ginger
Dried bonito flakes (optional)

Preparation
Cook the noodles as per the package's instructions. Sauté the pork slices in a cooking pan until brown. Then stir in the vegetables and sauté until soft. Add the noodles, Yakisoba sauce, mayonnaise, and mix well. Finally, garnish with seaweed, ginger, and bonito flakes. Serve warm.

Chaikin Tofu in Ginger Broth

Preparation time: 10 minutes
Cook time: 33 minutes
Nutrition facts (per serving): 242 cal (5g fat, 7g protein, 2g fiber)

If you haven't tried the Chaikin tofu before, then here comes a simple and easy to cook recipe that you can recreate at home in no time with minimum efforts.

Ingredients (4 servings)
⅔ lb. (400 g) block firm tofu, diced
¼ teaspoon dried wakame seaweed
7 oz. (200 g) minced chicken breast
1 teaspoon soy sauce
1 tablespoon of sake
1 egg white
1 ⅔ oz. (50 g) carrot, chopped
3 spring onions, chopped
2 teaspoon ginger, grated
1 tablespoon corn starch
1 teaspoon baking powder
1 pinch of salt and white pepper

Ginger broth
3 cups (750 ml) dashi stock
3 tablespoon soy sauce
2 tablespoons sake
2 tablespoon mirin
4 shallots, sliced
1 tablespoon corn starch mixed with 1 tablespoon water

Preparation

Soak the dried wakame in cold water for 10 minutes, drain, and chop. Mix the chicken with the egg white, sake, and soy sauce in a large bowl. Stir in the carrot, tofu, spring onions, wakame, cornstarch, baking powder, black pepper, salt, and 1 teaspoon grated ginger. Mix well to coat. Layer a rice bowl with cling film and divide the tofu mixture in them. Wrap them in the cling and place the parcels in the steamer for 20 minutes on medium-low heat. Meanwhile, boil the dashi stock in a saucepan. Add the mirin, sake, and soy sauce and cook for 4 minutes. Add the salt, white pepper, and shallots and then cook for 2 minutes. Stir in the corn starch and cook for 20 seconds with occasional stirring. Remove the steamed tofu parcels from the cling film and place them in a bowl. Divide the parcels in the bowls and pour the broth on top. Garnish with ginger. Serve warm.

Kabocha Pumpkin Curry

Preparation time: 10 minutes
Cook time: 35 minutes
Nutrition facts (per serving): 610 cal (45g fat, 26g protein, 2g fiber)

Try cooking a delicious kabocha pumpkin curry with some unique combination of beef and pumpkin mix at home to enjoy the best of the Japanese flavors at home.

Ingredients (4 servings)
7 oz. (200 g) minced beef
5 oz. (150 g) kabocha pumpkin, peeled and diced
½ onion, diced
1 carrot, diced
3 cubes of Japanese curry roux
1-2 tablespoon vegetable oil
⅔ cup (150 ml) water
1 tablespoon cooking sake or wine
11 oz. (320 g) cooked rice
1 bay leaf

Preparation
Sauté the beef with oil in a soup pot until brown. Then add all the vegetables. Stir in curry cubes, sake, and water. Next, mix well. Add the bay leaf and cook for 15 minutes. Toss the pumpkin slices with 1 tablespoon vegetable oil on a baking sheet and bake for 15 minutes in the oven. Divide the rice in the serving bowls, pour the curry on top, and place the pumpkin slices on top. Serve warm.

Shogayaki Ginger Pork

Preparation time: 10 minutes
Cook time: 20 minutes
Nutrition facts (per serving): 406 cal (5g fat, 24g protein, 2g fiber)

Ginger pork sautéed with onion and sauces is loved by all, as this stir-fry makes your meal healthy. Serve warm with flatbread.

Ingredients (4 servings)
⅔ oz. (100 g) fresh ginger root, minced
5 ⅓ oz. (250 g) sliced pork
¼ onion, chopped
2 tablespoon soy sauce
2 tablespoon cooking sake
2 tablespoon mirin
1 teaspoon sugar
10 ½ oz. (300 g) cooked rice
¼ head cabbage, julienned

Preparation
Mix the sake, soy sauce, mirin, and sugar in a bowl. Stir in the ginger and pork, and then mix well to coat. Marinate the pork for 10 minutes. Sauté the onion with oil in a frying pan until soft. Stir in the pork, ginger, and its marinade. Finally, cook until the meat is brown. Add the rest of the ingredients and serve warm.

Sukiyaki Hot Pot

Preparation time: 10 minutes
Cook time: 17 minutes
Nutrition facts (per serving): 354 cal (11g fat, 57g protein, 5g fiber)

Sukiyaki hot pot is one delicious way to complete your Japanese menu; here's a recipe that you can try to have a delicious meal.

Ingredients (4 servings)
1 cup (250 ml) sukiyaki sauce
3 ½ oz. (100 g) shirataki noodles
1 pack tofu, diced
11 oz. (320 g) Japanese rice
10 ½ oz. (300 g) sukiyaki beef, diced
1 pack enoki mushrooms, diced
6 rehydrated shiitake mushrooms, diced
1 spring onion, chopped
½ Chinese cabbage (Hokusai)
4 boiled eggs, peeled and cut in half

Preparation
Sauté the beef with oil in a cooking pan until golden brown. Stir in the sauce, tofu, mushrooms, and cabbage and then cook for 5-7 minutes. Divide the rice into the serving bowls with the beef-tofu mixture and eggs. Serve warm.

Horse Mackerel with Vegetables

Preparation time: 10 minutes
Cook time: 18 minutes
Nutrition facts (per serving): 240 cal (3.1g fat, 31g protein, 14g fiber)

Let's make horse mackerel with vegetables and these simple ingredients. Mix them together, and then cook to achieve great flavors.

Ingredients (3 servings)
3 horse mackerel fillets
1 onion, julienned
1 carrot, julienned
2 bell peppers, julienned
3 tablespoon potato starch
1 pinch of salt and black pepper
Oil for frying

Marinade
3 ¼ tablespoon (50 ml) sushi vinegar
1 tablespoon mirin rice wine
1 tablespoon sake
1 ½ tablespoon soy sauce
1 red chili pepper, dried

Preparation
Mix the vinegar, rice wine, sake, soy sauce, and red chili pepper in a bowl and add the mackerel fillets. Rub the marinade on top and cover to marinate the fish for 10 minutes. Sauté the vegetables with oil in a cooking pan for 5 minutes, then remove them from the heat. Coat the fish with potato starch, black pepper, and salt. Heat the oil for frying in a pan at 350 degrees F and sear the fish for 3 minutes per side. Serve warm with the sautéed veggies.

Mushroom Risotto with Grapefruit Duck Breast

Preparation time: 10 minutes
Cook time: 45 minutes
Nutrition facts (per serving): 486 cal (35.4 g fat, 33g protein, 1g fiber)

Count on this Japanese Mushroom Risotto to make your dinner extra special and surprise your loved one with the ultimate flavors.

Ingredients (4 servings)
⅔ cup (150 ml) gekkeikan sake
2 duck breast fillets with skin on
5 oz. (140 g) risotto rice
2 oz. (60 g) shitake mushrooms, sliced
1 oz. (30 g) dried oyster mushrooms, soaked and sliced
½ fennel bulb, sliced
3 shallots, diced
Juice of ½ lemon
½ red grapefruit, segmented
4 garlic cloves, diced
2 bay leaves
1 chicken stock cube mixed with 1 cup hot water
1 Romano cauliflower
2 tablespoon grated Parmesan
⅔ oz. (100 g) butter
1 tablespoon rapeseed oil
1 pinch of salt and black pepper

Preparation
Sauté the shallots and garlic with butter and oil in a cooking pan until soft. Stir in the fennel and bay leaves. Next, cover to cook for 5 minutes. Add the rice and sauté for 5 minutes. Pour in the sake and cook for 5 minutes. Add the mushrooms and their liquor and then cook for 5 minutes. Pour in the chicken

stock and cook until liquid is absorbed. Top the risotto with parmesan cheese and cover. Leave it until the cheese is melted. Pour in the lemon juice and give the rice a stir. Score the duck and season it with black pepper and salt. Sear the duck in a pan greased with cooking oil until golden brown. Toss in the grapefruit segments and cook for 1 minute per side.

Add a splash of sake and squeeze the grapefruit juice lightly. Cook for 4 minutes, cover the mixture with a foil, and then leave it for 5 minutes. Steam the cauliflower florets in a steamer for 4 minutes. Sauté the steamed florets and mushrooms with butter in a pan until golden brown. Divide the risotto in the serving plates, d top it with duck breasts and grapefruits juice, and serve with the veggie mix on the side. Serve warm.

Chicken and Tomato Nimono Stew

Preparation time: 10 minutes
Cook time: 35 minutes
Nutrition facts (per serving): 421 cal (11g fat, 29.5g protein, 2g fiber)

This chicken and tomato Nimono stew will melt your heart away with its epic flavors. This stew is filled with different spices and sauces that you can easily get and cook.

Ingredients (4 servings)
⅔ lb. (400 g) chopped tomatoes
7 oz. (200 g) chicken breast, diced
1 cup (200 ml) water
1 tablespoon sugar
1 tablespoon soy sauce
1 tablespoon mirin
1 teaspoon garlic paste
3 ¼ tablespoon (50 ml) red wine
1 bay leaf
2 tablespoon tomato ketchup
1 stock cube

Preparation
Sauté the chicken in a saucepan over medium heat until brown. Stir in the wine, water, bay leaf, wine, and tomatoes. Next, cook for 15 minutes on medium heat. Add all remaining ingredients and cook for 15 minutes. Serve warm.

Lamb Loin with Mung Bean

Preparation time: 10 minutes
Cook time: 10 minutes
Nutrition facts (per serving): 433 cal (1.3g fat, 34g protein, 1g fiber)

If you haven't tried the Japanese lamb loin with mung bean before, then here comes a simple and easy to cook recipe that you can recreate at home in no time with minimum efforts.

Ingredients (2 servings)
⅔ lb. (400 g) lamb loin, sliced
1 onion, sliced
1 carrot, sliced
3 ½ oz. (100 g) moyashi mung bean sprouts
½ tablespoon vegetable oil

Marinade
½ onion
½ apple, peeled and cored
1 garlic clove
⅔ oz. (100 g) fresh ginger root, peeled
5 tablespoon soy sauce
2 tablespoon cooking sake
2 tablespoon orange juice
1 tablespoon sugar
¼ teaspoon pepper

Preparation
Mix the onion, ginger, garlic, mung bean sprouts, and apple in a large bowl. Stir in the orange juice, black pepper, sugar, sake, and soy sauce and then mix well. Add the lamb slices and mix well to coat, cover and marinate for 15 minutes.

Sauté the veggies and lamb mixture with vegetable oil and cook for 5-10 minutes. Serve warm.

Sesame Salmon with Coconut Rice

Preparation time: 15 minutes
Cook time: 40 minutes
Nutrition facts (per serving): 312 cal (9g fat, 23g protein, 0.5g fiber)

The famous Sesame salmon recipe is here to make your Japanese cuisine extra special. Serve it with coconut rice for the best taste.

Ingredients (4 servings)
Sesame salmon
4 salmon fillets, bones removed
1 tablespoon of honey
½ tablespoon of soy sauce
1 red chili, sliced
1 knob of fresh ginger, grated
2 tablespoon of sesame oil

Pickled cucumber
½ cucumber, sliced lengthways into ribbons
4 tablespoon of rice wine vinegar
1 tablespoon of caster sugar
½ cup (125ml) of water
½ teaspoon cumin seeds
½ teaspoon coriander seeds
1 teaspoon nigella seeds

Coconut rice
1 ½ cup (400 ml) of coconut milk
1 ½ cup (400 ml) of water, boiling
⅔ lb. (400 g) of akafuji akitakomachi rice

Serve

4 oz. (120 g) of edamame
1 tablespoon of toasted sesame seeds
1 handful of pea shoots

Preparation

Mix the vinegar, sugar, and ½ cup (125ml) water in a small saucepan and cook until sugar is dissolved. Allow this mixture to cool and then add cumin seeds and coriander. Pour this mixture into a sterilized jar and add the cucumber. Cover and refrigerate the cucumber for 4 hours. Add the rice and coconut milk to a saucepan and cook for 10 minutes with occasional stirring. Remove the rice from the heat and cover and, then leave them aside. Mix the sesame oil, ginger, chili, soy sauce, and honey in a bowl. Add the salmon fillets to the sauce and rub over. Leave them for 15 minutes. Set a grill over medium heat and grill the salmon for 5 minutes per side. Boil the edamame in water using a small pan for 5 minutes, then drain. Divide these beans and rice into the serving bowls. Top them with grilled salmon and pickled cucumber. Garnish with sesame seeds and pea shoots. Serve.

Oyster Gratin with Tofu Sauce

Preparation time: 10 minutes
Cook time: 23 minutes
Nutrition facts (per serving): 470 cal (12g fat, 24g protein, 6 g fiber)

This Japanese oyster gratin with tofu sauce recipe has unique flavors due to its rich blend of oysters with a cheesy topping. Serve warm with rice or bread.

Ingredients (2 servings)
½ pack of silken tofu
1 tablespoon milk
1 teaspoon consommé stock powder
3 ½ oz. (100 g) oysters
½ onion
2 tablespoons cheese for topping
5 g powdered cheese
1 teaspoon shio koji seasoning
1 pinch of salt and black pepper

Preparation
Blend the cheese, consommé powder, milk, tofu, and shio koji in a food processor until smooth. Sauté the onion with butter in a cooking pan until soft. Stir in the oysters, black pepper, and salt and then cook for 3 minutes. Stir in the tofu mixture and cook until warm. Then spread them in a casserole fish. Spread the cheese on top and bake for 15 minutes at 320 degrees F. Serve warm.

Miso Marinated Pork Roast

Preparation time: 10 minutes
Cook time: 8 minutes
Nutrition facts (per serving): 419 cal (12g fat, 32g protein, 1g fiber)

Best to serve at dinner, this miso pork roast can be served as an energizing meal. Here's a Japanese version of delicious roast.

Ingredients (2 servings)
4 oz. (120 g) slice pork roast, 10mm thick
1 ½ oz. (40 g) hard or semi-hard cheese
1 ⅔ oz. (50 g) miso

Preparation
Rub the miso over the pork roast and wrap the pork with cling film and refrigerate overnight for 3 days. Place the pork slices in a preheated grill and cook for 4 minutes. Flip the pork and place the cheese slices on top. And grill for 4 minutes. Serve warm.

Matcha-Smoked Chicken

Preparation time: 15 minutes
Cook time: 63 minutes
Nutrition facts (per serving): 319cal (14g fat, 26g protein, 7g fiber)

Japanese Match smoked chicken is one good option to go for in dinner. Sure, it takes some time to get it ready, but it's a great taste is totally worth all the time and effort.

Ingredients (3 servings)
3 chicken breasts, skin-on

Brine
4 cups boiling water
1 ⅔ oz. (50 g) coarse sea salt
1 tablespoon matcha
1 ⅔ oz. (50 g) honey
½ tablespoon black peppercorns, crushed

To smoke
1 ⅔ oz. (50 g) rice, any variety
1 oz. (30 g) caster sugar
⅔ oz. (100 g) light brown sugar
1 tablespoon matcha

Salad
5 oz. (150 g) brown rice
7 oz. (200 g) green beans, trimmed and cut into 2-inch pieces
2 mangoes, just-ripe
4 tablespoon fresh mint, chopped
4 tablespoon fresh coriander, chopped
2 red chilies, deseeded and chopped
Lime, cut into wedges

Dressing

3 tablespoon rice vinegar
1 lime, zested and juiced
3 tablespoon groundnut oil or rapeseed oil
1 tablespoon ginger, grated
1 garlic clove, crushed
1 teaspoon fish sauce
2 teaspoon honey

Preparation

Mix boiling water with peppercorns, honey, 1 tablespoon matcha, and salt in a bowl. Pierce the chicken with a sharp knife and place the chicken in the brine. Cover and refrigerate for 3 hours. Remove the chicken from the brine and rinse it. Prepare a smoker and add the remaining matcha, sugar, and rice to its bottom tray. Place the chicken on the middle rack of the smoker and cover to smoke for 35 minutes on medium-low heat. Cook the brown rice with boiling water in a pan for 25 minutes, then drain and allow them to cool. Boil the green beans in boiling water for 3 minutes, then rinse and drain. Peel the mangoes and cut the flesh into slices. Transfer the mango to a salad bowl. Stir in the mint, green beans, chilies, coriander, and brown rice. Mix the dressing ingredients in a bowl, pour over the salad, and then mix well. Stir in the rice mixture and then mix well. Divide the salad in the serving plate and top it with chicken breasts. Garnish with coriander leaves and lime wedges. Serve warm.

Sesame Chicken

Preparation time: 15 minutes
Cook time: 25 minutes
Nutrition facts (per serving): 376 cal (14g fat, 22g protein, 18g fiber)

This sesame chicken recipe will make your day with a delightful taste. Serve warm with your favorite bread.

Ingredients (2 servings)
⅔ lb. (400 g) chicken breast, cut into chunks
½ tablespoon cooking sake
½ teaspoon sugar
1 pinch of salt
½ tablespoon mayonnaise
1 tablespoon katakuriko potato starch
3 tablespoon black and white sesame seeds
Sesame oil to drizzle

Preparation
Mix the chicken cubes with sake, sugar, salt, mayonnaise, potato starch in a bowl and transfer to a plastic bag. Seal the bag and coat well. Spread the chicken on a baking sheet and drizzle sesame seeds on top. Lastly, bake for 25 minutes at 360 degrees F. Serve warm.

Aubergine Miso Stir Fry

Preparation time: 15 minutes
Cook time: 8 minutes
Nutrition facts (per serving): 349 cal (7g fat, 9g protein, 3g fiber)

If you want some new flavors in your meals, this aubergine or eggplant miso stir fry recipe is best to bring variety to the menu.

Ingredients (4 servings)
1 aubergine or eggplant, sliced
1 green pepper, sliced
2 tablespoon mirin
1 ½ tablespoon tsuyu soup base
2 oz. (60 g) miso
1 oz. (30 g) ginger, grated
1 oz. (30 g) sugar

Preparation
Mix the mirin, soup base, miso, ginger, and sugar in a bowl. Sauté the aubergine/eggplant in a cooking pan for 4 minutes until brown, and then stir in pepper. Sauté for 3 minutes until soft, then stir in miso sauce, and cook for 2 minutes. Serve warm.

Miso Chicken Teriyaki

Preparation time: 5 minutes
Cook time: 13 minutes
Nutrition facts (per serving): 331 cal (11g fat, 30g protein, 0.3g fiber)

Here's a special Japanese chicken teriyaki, which is great to serve at special dinners and celebrations. The chicken is cooked with miso and green beans to make a delicious meal.

Ingredients (2 servings)
7 oz. (200 g) chicken thigh fillets, boneless
8 green beans, boiled
2 tablespoon liquid miso with dashi
2 tablespoon water
1 teaspoon vegetable oil
1 pinch of salt and black pepper

Preparation
Rub the chicken with black pepper and salt. Add oil to a cooking pan and sear the chicken in the oil for 5 minutes per side until golden brown. Mix 2 tablespoon water and miso in a bowl. Pour this mixture on top of the chicken. Add the green beans and cook for 3 minutes. Slice the chicken into strips and serve warm with rice.

Taki Komi Rice Pilaf

Preparation time: 15 minutes
Cook time: 20 minutes
Nutrition facts (per serving): 411 cal (9g fat, 21g protein, 7g fiber)

When you can't think of anything to serve in lunch or dinner, then this Taki Komi Rice pilaf will help you to enjoy the authentic Japanese flavors.

Ingredients (2 servings)
1 ½ tablespoon liquid miso with dashi
5 oz. (150 g) Japanese rice, rinsed
1 cup (200 ml) water
1 ⅔ oz. (50 g) chicken thigh, diced
⅔ oz. (25 g) shimeji mushrooms
⅛ carrot, sliced into rounds
¼ piece of aburaage fried tofu, cut into cubes
1 pinch of salt and black pepper
1 teaspoon vegetable oil
1 green onion, sliced

Preparation
Sauté the chicken with oil in a cooking pan on medium heat until golden brown for 4 minutes. Stir in the fried tofu, carrot, and shimeji and sauté until the tofu is golden brown. Add the rice and, water. Cook until the rice is done and garnish with green onion. Serve warm.

Aubergine Somen Noodles

Preparation time: 10 minutes
Cook time: 15 minutes
Nutrition facts (per serving): 326 cal (17g fat, 4g protein, 1.2g fiber)

Here's another classic recipe for your dinner and lunch collection. Serve it with a delicious entree and enjoy the best of it.

Ingredients (2 servings)
1 bundle somen noodles
½ aubergine or eggplant
⅓ cucumber
2 Shiso perilla leaves
1 teaspoon white sesame seeds
½ cup (100 ml) diluted tsuyu noodle soup base

Preparation
Grill the aubergine or eggplant in a grill over medium heat for 5 minutes per side. Cut the aubergine into wedges. Boil the noodles as per the package's instructions. Heat the soup base in a saucepan. Stir in the aubergine/eggplant, cucumber, perilla leaves, and noodles. Then cook for 2 minutes. Garnish with sesame seeds. Serve warm.

Desserts

Sakura Cherry Blossom Swiss Roll

Preparation time: 10 minutes
Cook time: 23 minutes
Nutrition facts (per serving): 271 cal (7g fat, 6g protein, 2g fiber)

If you haven't tried the famous Japanese cherry blossom Swiss roll, then here comes a simple and easy to cook recipe that you can recreate at home in no time with minimum efforts.

Ingredients (6 servings)
Sponge
1 oz. (30 g) flour
1 oz. (30 g) rice flour, joshinko
3 eggs, separated
2 oz. (60 g) sugar
2 tablespoon vegetable oil
4 teaspoon (20 ml) milk
⅔ oz. (25 g) cherry blossom bean paste
Red food coloring

Syrup
1 teaspoon sugar
1 tablespoon hot water

Cream filling
5 ½ tablespoon (80 ml) whipping cream
4 teaspoon (20 ml) condensed milk
2 ⅔ oz. sakura-a cherry blossom bean paste

Preparation
Beat the egg whites in a bowl until it makes soft peaks and stir in half of the sugar. Next, whip well until it makes a meringue. Beat the egg yolks with the remaining

sugar in a bowl for 3 minutes until they turn pale in color. Stir in the milk, vegetable oil, sakura-an, and food coloring, then mix well. Stir in the rice flour and flour, and then mix until smooth. Stir in half of the egg white meringue and mix gently. Add the remaining meringue and mix only until evenly combined. Layer a baking sheet with parchment paper and spread the prepared batter into this sheet, and bake for 20 minutes at 320 degrees F. Meanwhile, prepare the syrup by mixing sugar with hot water in a saucepan. Allow the baked sponge cake to cool and brush the syrup on top. Beat the cream in a bowl until it makes soft peaks. Stir in the condensed milk, and then beat until fluffy. Spread this mixture over the sponge while leaving ½ inch around the edges. Add sakura-an on top. Roll the sponge cake while wrapping the parchment paper around. Slice and serve.

Fluffy Japanese Pancakes

Preparation time: 15 minutes
Cook time: 12 minutes
Nutrition facts (per serving): 174 cal (4g fat, 6g protein, 1g fiber)

Do you want to enjoy pancakes with a Japanese twist? Then try these fluffiest Japanese pancakes with this simple recipe. You can serve them with your favorite dips and sauces.

Ingredients (4 servings)

5 oz. (150 g) self-rising flour
½ teaspoon baking powder
2 tablespoon golden caster sugar
2 eggs
1 tablespoon rapeseed oil
⅔ cup (180 ml) milk
1 dash of vanilla extract
Oil spray for cooking
Maple syrup, ice cream, crisp bacon, berries

Preparation

Mix flour with baking powder and sugar in a bowl. Make a well at the center of this mixture. Add the oil and the eggs to the center and mix gradually while adding milk. Stir in vanilla and mix until smooth. Set a pan over low heat and set 1-2 crumpet rings in the pan. Spray them with oil and pour the batter into the rings. Cover the pan's lid and cook for 10 minutes on low heat. Flip the pancakes and cook for 2 minutes. Serve.

Ganache Filled Strawberry Daifuku

Preparation time: 15 minutes
Cook time: 3 minutes
Nutrition facts (per serving): 148 cal (1g fat, 7g protein, 2g fiber)

Here's a beloved dessert that has no parallel, as the Japanese Daifuku is made with soft and moist cake rice wrap filled with matcha ganache and strawberry.

Ingredients (6 servings)

6 fresh strawberries, stems trimmed off
3 ½ oz. (100 g) rice flour or shiratamako
⅔ oz. (100 g) sugar
⅔ cup (150 ml) water
Corn flour for dusting

Matcha ganache
3 tablespoon double cream
2 teaspoon matcha powder
5 oz. (150 g) white chocolate

Preparation

Mix the double cream and the white chocolate in a bowl. Place this bowl in a saucepan filled with boiling water and place it over low heat. Cook until the chocolate is melted. Mix water with matcha powder in a bowl until lump-free. Stir in melted chocolate and mix well. Insert a wooden stick into each strawberry and dip in the ganache. Mix rice flour with sugar in a bowl, then stir in water and mix until smooth.

Heat this rice flour dough for 1 minute in the microwave. Mix and heat again for 1 minute in the microwave until thickens. Mix and heat again for 30 seconds in the microwave. Dust a working surface with corn flour and transfer the dough onto it. Divide the dough into six equal portions. Roll and spread each portion into 3 inches round circle. Place one coated strawberry at the center of each dough circle and wrap it around the strawberry. Serve.

Strawberry Awayukikan Dessert

Preparation time: 15 minutes
Cook time: 10 minutes
Nutrition facts (per serving): 221 cal (3 g fat, 4g protein, 2.8g fiber)

Yes, you can make something as delicious as this Awayukikan dessert by using only basic ingredients using some simple techniques.

Ingredients (4 servings)
5 strawberries
1 ¼ cups (300 ml) water
2 teaspoon powdered Kanten agar-agar
1 egg white
1 ⅔ oz. (50 g) sugar

Preparation
Mash three strawberries in a bowl with a fork and slice the rest for garnishing. Mix the gelatin with water in a saucepan over medium heat and cook until the gelatin is dissolved. Stir in the mashed strawberries and sugar, mix well, and then remove it from the heat. Allow the mixture to cool. Beat the egg white in a bowl until it gets stiff peaks, and then fold in gelatin mixture. Layer a baking pan with parchment paper and place the strawberry in the baking pan. Pour the gelatin mixture on top and spread evenly. Refrigerate the dessert for 2 hours. Flip the pan over the serving platter and slice to serve.

Strawberry and Red Bean Paste Dorayaki

Preparation time: 15 minutes
Cook time: 24 minutes
Nutrition facts (per serving): 217 cal (13g fat, 5g protein, 0.2g fiber)

Try this Japanese red bean dorayaki on the menu. The sweet combination of red bean paste with strawberries is bliss for all the sweet tooth fans like I am!

Ingredients (4 servings)

5 oz. (150 g) pancake mix
2 eggs
1 ½ tablespoon sugar
2 tablespoon honey
1 ½ tablespoon mirin
½ cup (100 ml) milk

Fillings

5 oz. (150 g) Anko sweet red bean paste
Fresh strawberries

Preparation

Beat the eggs with mirin, honey, and sugar in a bowl. Stir in milk and mix well. Place a sieve on top and pass the pancake mix through the sieve. Mix well until smooth. Place a frying pan over medium heat and pour a ladle of this batter into the pan. Cook the pancake for 2-3 minutes per side until golden brown. Cook more pancakes using the remaining batter and then transfer to a plate. Top the pancakes with sweet red bean paste and strawberries. Fold the pancakes and serve.

Strawberry Amazake Pudding

Preparation time: 10 minutes
Cook time: 7 minutes
Nutrition facts (per serving): 225 cal (17g fat, 5g protein, 0.8g fiber)

This Japanese Amazake pudding will leave you spellbound due to its mildly sweet taste and the combination of amazake pudding topped with strawberry sauces.

Ingredients (4 servings)
Pudding
1 cup (240 ml) amazake
1 cup (240 ml) milk
1 ½ tablespoon condensed milk
¼ oz. powdered gelatin (agar kanten)

Strawberry sauce
6 strawberries
1 tablespoon sugar
½ teaspoon lemon juice

Topping
4 strawberries

Preparation
Mix the amazake with condensed milk and milk in a saucepan and place it over medium heat. Bring this mixture to a boil. Mix 1 tablespoon cold water and gelatin in a bowl. Pour this mixture into the milk mixture and stir well. Allow the milk to cool down for 10 minutes. Divide the milk pudding into four serving glasses and refrigerate for 4 hours. Meanwhile, prepare the strawberry sauce. Add sugar, lemon juice, and strawberries to a bowl and heat for 2 minutes in the

microwave. Mash the strawberries with a spoon and then allow the sauce to cool. Pour the sauce on top of the pudding. Garnish and serve.

Yuzu Matcha Truffles

Preparation time: 15 minutes
Cook time: 15 minutes
Nutrition facts (per serving): 77 cal (4g fat, 1g protein, 4g fiber)

The famous yuzu matcha truffles are essential to try on the Japanese dessert menu. Try cooking on your own with these healthy ingredients and enjoy it.

Ingredients (12 servings)
Yuzu white chocolate ganache
3 ½ oz. (100 g) double cream
6 oz. (175 g) good quality white chocolate
1-3 tablespoon yuzu juice

White chocolate and matcha coating
10 ½ oz. (300 g) good quality white chocolate
⅔ oz. (100 g) matcha powder

Preparation
Boil cream in a pan, and then remove from the heat. Break the chocolate and add the pieces to a bowl. Pour the cream over the chocolate and mix well until chocolate melts. Stir in one tablespoon yuzu juice and continue mixing. Spread this ganache in a baking sheet and cover with a cling film, and place in the refrigerator for 30 minutes. Take a spoonful of the ganache and roll it into a ball. Make more balls with the rest of the ganache. Melt the remaining white chocolate in a bowl by heating in the microwave and dip the balls in the white chocolate. Then roll them in the matcha powder. Place the truffles on a baking sheet for 15 minutes. Serve.

Strawberry and Sweet Red Bean Mochi (Ichigo Daifuku)

Preparation time: 10 minutes
Cook time: 3 minutes
Nutrition facts (per serving): 108 cal (20g fat, 4g protein, 0.4g fiber)

If you want something exotic on your dessert menu, then nothing can taste better than this delicious strawberry and red bean mochi.

Ingredients (6 servings)
2 ⅔ oz. shiratama rice flour
½ cup (120 ml) water
6 strawberries
6 oz. (180 g) red bean paste
2 tablespoon Katakuriko starch powder
⅔ oz. (100 g) sugar

Preparation
Wrap each strawberry with red bean paste. Mix the rice flour with water in a bowl, then stirs in sugar. Cover this bowl with cling film and heat the mixture in the microwave for 2 minutes. Mix and add a teaspoon of water if the dough is too solid. Cover again with a cling film and cook for 1 minute. Drizzle Katakuriko in a flat tray. Place the dough in this tray and flatten it. Roll the dough and divide into 6 portions. Flatten each portion and wrap each around one strawberry-red bean paste ball. Serve.

Matcha Soy Milk And Azuki Pudding

Preparation time: 10 minutes
Cook time: 3 minutes
Nutrition facts (per serving): 193 cal (18g g fat, 9g protein, 3g fiber)

The famous azuki pudding is another special dessert to try on the Japanese menu. Try cooking it at home with these healthy ingredients and enjoy it.

Ingredients (2 servings)
1 ½ cup (400 ml) unsweetened soy milk
2 tablespoon castor sugar
⅓ oz. (10 g) gelatin powder or gelatin leaves
2 tablespoon matcha powder
4 tablespoons cooked sweet azuki beans

Preparation
Add the gelatin, sugar, and soy milk to a saucepan and place over low heat. Mix well and cook until the gelatin is melted, then remove it from the heat. Mix the matcha powder with 1 tablespoon hot water in a bowl until it makes a smooth paste. Transfer this paste to the soy milk and mix well. Add 1 tablespoon azuki beans to each of the four-serving bowls. Divide the matcha mixture on top. Allow the pudding to cool and refrigerate for 1 hour. Garnish with cream, matcha powder, and chocolate flakes. Serve.

Yuzu Cupcakes with Matcha Frosting

Preparation time: 15 minutes
Cook time: 22 minutes
Nutrition facts (per serving): 101cal (6g fat, 4g protein, 0.6g fiber)

The Japanese yuzu cupcakes have no parallel; these cupcakes are topped with a delicious blend of matcha frosting.

Ingredients (6 servings)
Cupcakes
3 ¾ oz. (110 g) butter softened
3 ¾ oz. (110 g) caster sugar
2 eggs, beaten
3 ¾ oz. (110 g) self-rising flour
1 tablespoon milk

Frosting
3 ¼ tablespoon (50 ml) water
⅔ cup (150 ml) granulated sugar
2 egg whites
¼ teaspoon cream of tartar
1 pinch salt
½ teaspoon vanilla
1 tablespoon fine matcha powder

Yuzu syrup
1 oz. (30 g) sugar
6 teaspoon (30 ml) water
6 teaspoon (30 ml) yuzu juice

Garnish
Sprinkles and nonpareils

Preparation
At 350 degrees F, preheat your oven. Layer a 12-cup muffin tray with paper liners. Beat the sugar with butter in a bowl until it is pale. Add the eggs and beat well. Stir in the flour and mix until smooth. Divide the batter into the muffin cups and bake for 15 minutes until golden brown. Allow the muffins to cool on a wire rack. Meanwhile, mix the cream of tartar, salt, egg whites, sugar, tea, and water in a bowl and then place this bowl in a saucepan filled with boiling water. Mix the frosting with an electric whisk for 7 minutes, and then remove it from the heat. Allow the frosting to cool. Mix water and sugar in a pan for the yuzu syrup. Mix and cook this mixture on low heat. Stir in the juice and mix well. Allow the syrup to cool, and then pour over all the cupcakes. Pipe the frosting on top of the cupcakes and garnish. Serve.

Gugelhupf Cake

Preparation time: 10 minutes
Cook time: 20 minutes
Nutrition facts (per serving): 203 cal (7g fat, 3g protein, 1g fiber)

The Gugelhupf cake is great to serve with all the hot beverages, and it's popular for the sweet and earthy taste.

Ingredients (6 servings)

3 ½ oz. (100 g) pancake mix
1 oz. (30 g) sugar
1 egg
4 tablespoon (60 ml) milk
Sultanas
Candied peel
Almonds

Preparation

At 350 degrees F, preheat your oven. Grease a Bundt cake pan with butter. Spread the almonds at the bottom of this pan. Mix the sugar with the pancake mix in a bowl. Beat in the milk and egg, and then mix for 1 minute. Dust the sultanas and candied peel with flour and then add to the batter. Pour the batter into the Bundt pan and bake for 20 minutes. Allow the cake to cool and slice to serve.

Kashiwa Mochi

Preparation time: 10 minutes
Cook time: 7 minutes
Nutrition facts (per serving): 168 cal (1.4g fat, 1g protein, 2g fiber)

The Japanese Kashiwa mochis wrapped in oak leaves is worth the try as they taste so unique and exotic. This dessert is definitely a must on the Japanese menu.

Ingredients (8 servings)
7 oz. (200 g) azuki sweet red beans
7 oz. (200 g) joshinko rice flour
1 ¼ cups (280 ml) water
8 oak leaves

Preparation
Heat the azuki in a pan on low heat until it thickens and then remove it from the heat. Mix the rice flour and water in a bowl. Cover and heat the mixture for 4 minutes in the microwave. Mix well and heat again for 3 minutes in the microwave. Allow the dough to cool and knead it on a working surface. Divide the dough into 8 equal portions. Flatten each dough piece. Divide the red bean paste on top of the flattened pieces. Fold the dough over the filling and seal the edges. Wrap each mochi ball with one oak leaf. Serve.

Mizu Manju with Azuki Bean Paste

Preparation time: 15 minutes
Cook time: 3 minutes
Nutrition facts (per serving): 189 cal (13g fat, 3g protein, 2g fiber)

If you haven't tried the Japanese Mizu Manju, then here comes a simple and easy to cook recipe that you can recreate at home in no time with minimum efforts.

Ingredients (12 servings)
1 ⅔ oz. (50 g) kuzu arrowroot starch
⅔ oz. (100 g) sugar
1 ⅓ cups (320 ml) water
8 ½ oz. (240 g) sweet azuki bean paste

Preparation
Mix the sugar with water in a bowl until dissolved. Then add the starch and kuzu. Mix until the mixture is lump-free. Transfer the mixture to a pan and cook for 3 minutes until it thickens, and then remove it from the heat. Allow it to cool. Divide the kuzu mixture into an ice-cube tray. Make small balls out of half of the bean paste. And place each ball in each ice cube. Use the remaining paste to cover the cubes and refrigerate for 2 hours. Serve.

Minazuki Rice Cake Topped With Azuki Beans

Preparation time: 15 minutes
Cook time: 30 minutes
Nutrition facts (per serving): 150 cal (6g fat, 2g protein, 0g fiber)

The famous Minazuki rice cake is essential to try on the Japanese dessert menu. Try cooking it at home with these healthy ingredients and enjoy it.

Ingredients (6 servings)
1 oz. (30 g) kuzu arrowroot starch
1 oz. (30 g) shiratamako rice flour
2 oz. (60 g) flour
2 oz. (60 g) sugar
1 cup (200 ml) water
3 ½ oz. (100 g) canned, boiled azuki sweet red beans, drained

Preparation
Mix the rice flour with arrowroot starch and water in a bowl until it makes a smooth paste. Add sugar and flour. Then mix until smooth. Rinse a 6x5 inch rectangular mold to wet it a little. Add half of the prepared mixture to this mold and steam it for 20 minutes in a steamer. Remove the cake from the mold. Add the red bean mixture on top of the cake and add the remaining cake batter on top. Return the mold to the steamer and steam again for 10 minutes. Allow the cake to cool and cut it into 12 pieces. Serve.

Japanese Kuri Youkan Chestnut Jelly Cake

Preparation time: 15 minutes
Cook time: 5 minutes
Nutrition facts (per serving): 128 cal (6g fat, 4g protein, 3g fiber)

Japanese Kuri Youkan Chestnut Jelly Cake is one good option to go for in the desserts. You can also keep them ready and stored and then use them readily as instant desserts.

Ingredients (6 servings)
1 can Kuri kanroni chestnuts in syrup, chopped
1 ⅔ oz. (50 g) azuki paste
⅓ oz. (10 g) kanten powdered agar
7 oz. (200 g) sugar
2 cups (470 ml) water

Preparation
Add water and kanten powder to a pan and cook over medium heat with stirring for 5 minutes. Stir in the sugar and mix until dissolved. Add the chestnuts and azuki paste. Then pour this mixture into a container and allow it to cool. Cover and refrigerate this cake for 2 hours. Slice and serve.

Tricolored Hishi Mochi

Preparation time: 10 minutes
Cook time: 3 minutes
Nutrition facts (per serving): 241 cal (4g fat, 2g protein, 1.1g fiber)

Here comes a dessert that is most loved by all. The walnut tartlets are not only served as a dessert, but are also a breakfast treat in Japan.

Ingredients (6 servings)
Green layer
1 ⅔ oz. (50 g) rice flour
1 ½ oz. (40 g) sugar
5 tablespoon (75ml) water
3 tablespoon matcha powder

White layer
1 ⅔ oz. (50 g) rice flour
1 ½ oz. (40 g) sugar
5 tablespoon (75ml) water

Pink layer
1 ⅔ oz. (50 g) rice flour
1 ½ oz. (40 g) sugar
5 tablespoon (75ml) water
Red food coloring
Potato starch powder, for dusting

Preparation
Mix all the green layer ingredients in a bowl and cover them with a cling film. Heat this green mixture in the microwave for 2 minutes. Give it a stir and heat again for 1 minute. Dust an 8x8 inch baking sheet with potato starch powder. Spread the green layer to cover the bottom of the baking sheet; use a rolling pin

if needed. Mix the white layer ingredients in a bowl and heat in the same manner, and then spread it on top of the green layer. Prepare the pink layer in the same way and spread on top. Drizzle the potato starch powder on top and leave the mochi for 30 minutes. Cut the layers into diamond-shaped pieces. Serve.

Three Color Dango Dumplings

Preparation time: 5 minutes
Nutrition facts (per serving): 112 cal (2g fat, 4 protein, 3g fiber)

Try the colorful Dango dumplings to adorn your dinner table with tempting hues and irresistible taste with this quick recipe.

Ingredients (1 serving)
5 oz. (160 g) joshinko rice flour
1 ½ oz. (40 g) shiratamako rice flour
2 oz. (60 g) sugar
1 cup (200 ml) hot water
1 teaspoon matcha green tea powder
Red food coloring

Preparation
Mix the rice flour, shiratamako rice flour, and hot water in a bowl. Cover this bowl and heat the rice-flour mixture for 3 minutes. Allow the dough to cool, and then knead the dough. Divide this dough into three portions, add food coloring to one portion, and then add the matcha powder to another portion. Divide each dough portion into 6 pieces and roll them into balls. Alternately thread, green, red, and white dough balls on bamboo skewers. Serve.

Drinks

Calpis Japanese Drink

Preparation time: 10 minutes
Nutrition facts (per serving): 140 cal (10g fat, 8g protein, 0.5g fiber)

Without this Calpis Japanese drink, it seems like the Japanese cocktail menu is incomplete. Try it with different variations of toppings.

Ingredients (1 serving)
½ cup Greek-style yogurt
3 tablespoon Lemon juice
2 oz. sugar
Mineral water/water/soda to dilute

Preparation
Whisk the yogurt with sugar and lemon juice in a container and cover to refrigerate. Mix ¼ yogurt mixture and ¾ cup of water to prepare and serve with mint leaves on top. Serve.

Japanese Slipper Cocktail

Preparation time: 10 minutes
Nutrition facts (per serving): 102 cal (7g fat, 1g protein, 1.3g fiber)

If you enjoy Midori flavors, then this Japanese cocktail is the right fit for you. Try this at home and prepare in no time.

Ingredients (1 serving)
1 oz. melon liqueur, Midori
1 oz. orange liqueur, Cointreau
1 oz. lemon juice

Garnish
Honeydew melon slice or ball

Preparation
All the cocktail ingredients to a cocktail shaker and shake well. Garnish with a honeydew melon slice. Serve.

Japanese Cream Soda

Preparation time: 5 minutes
Nutrition facts (per serving): 123cal (7g fat, 3g protein, 1g fiber)

The Japanese cream soda is loved by all due to its refreshing taste and sweet flavors. Serve it chilled for the best taste and flavor.

Ingredients (1 serving)
3 tablespoon melon syrup
Ice cubes
¾ cup club soda
Vanilla ice cream
Maraschino cherries

Preparation
Add the melon syrup, ice, and club soda to a cocktail shaker, and then shake well. Garnish with ice cream and cherries.

Sakuranbo Bitter

Preparation time: 10 minutes
Nutrition facts (per serving): 117 cal (0g fat, 0g protein, 0g fiber)

The Japanese Sakuranbo bitter is great to serve on all special occasions and dinner. Add the final touch with a refreshing orange peel on top.

Ingredients (1 serving)
3 ¼ tablespoon (50 ml) yuzu umeshu
6 teaspoon (30 ml) cherry brandy
1 ¾ tablespoon (25ml) Campari

Preparation
All the cocktail ingredients to a cocktail shaker and shake well. Serve.

Autumn Kaze

Preparation time: 10 minutes
Nutrition facts (per serving): 112 cal (13g fat, 3g protein, 1g fiber)

The Japanese Autumn Kaze is famous for its blend of Shochu, Jim beam whiskey, and Cointreau. You can prep this drink easily at home.

Ingredients (2 servings)
3 ¼ tablespoon (50 ml) bizan shochu
1 ¾ tablespoon (25ml) rye Jim beam whiskey
1 ¾ tablespoon (25ml) Cointreau
2 teaspoon (10 ml) yuzu umeshu
8 teaspoon (40 ml) cold espresso
1 tablespoon (15ml) homemade vanilla syrup
1 dash of orange angostura bitter
3 coffee beans and half of a vanilla pod for garnish

Preparation
Add the bizan, rye Jim, Cointreau, yuzu, cold espresso, angostura bitter, and vanilla syrup to a cocktail shaker and shake well. Pour this drink into a chilled coupe glass and garnish with coffee beans and vanilla pod.

Kaoru Lavender Cocktail

Preparation time: 5 minutes
Nutrition facts (per serving): 161 cal (0g fat, 0.7g protein, 1.4g fiber)

The Kaoru lavender cocktail is all that you need to celebrate the holidays. Keep the drink ready in your refrigerator for quick serving.

Ingredients (1 serving)
6 teaspoon (30 ml) St. Germain
1 ¾ tablespoon (25ml) Josen sake
1 ¾ tablespoon (25ml) jinzu gin
5 limes
½ small, peeled cucumber
1 teaspoon of brown sugar
1 pinch of dry lavender

Preparation
Add the cucumber, brown sugar, and lime to a bowl, crush and mix these ingredients together. Stir in ½ teaspoon dry lavender. Mix sake, gin, and St. Germain in a shaker. Pour the drink into a serving glass. Add ice and the crushed cucumber mixture. Serve.

Japan-no-cino

Preparation time: 5 minutes
Nutrition facts (per serving): 120 cal (0g fat, 1g protein, 1g fiber)

Here's a special Japanese drink made out of nigori sake, amaretto, Kahlua, and cold espresso, which is great to serve at special dinners and celebrations.

Ingredients (1 serving)
3 ¼ tablespoon (50 ml) nigori sake
6 teaspoon (30 ml) amaretto
4 teaspoon (20 ml) Kahlua
4 tablespoon (60 ml) cold espresso
Milk foam

Preparation
Shake the sake, amaretto, Kahlua, and cold espresso with a cocktail shaker. Serve with milk foam on top.

Hokkaido Ice

Preparation time: 5 minutes
Nutrition facts (per serving): 152 cal (13g fat, 12g protein, 2.3g fiber)

Made out of Josen sake, blue curacao, Frangelico, and coconut milk, this beverage is a refreshing addition to the Japanese cocktail menu.

Ingredients (1 serving)
4 tablespoon (60 ml) Josen sake
8 teaspoon (40 ml) blue curacao
6 teaspoon (30 ml) Frangelico
4 teaspoon (20 ml) coconut milk

Preparation
Shake the sake, blue curacao, Frangelico, and coconut milk in a cocktail shaker. Serve.

Niseko Sparkle

Preparation time: 10 minutes
Nutrition facts (per serving): 120 cal (0g fat, 0g protein, 0.3g fiber)

This refreshing Japanese cocktail is always a delight to serve at parties. Now you can make it easily at home by using the following simple ingredients.

Ingredients (1 serving)
1 tablespoon (50 ml) sake with gold flakes
1 teaspoon raisins
6 teaspoon (30 ml) Absolut pear vodka
8 teaspoon (40 ml) pear juice
4 teaspoon (20 ml) Benedictine
2 teaspoon (10 ml) grenadine syrup

Preparation
Mix the raisins with the sake in a bowl for 2 hours, and then transfer to a food processor. Add the pear vodka, pear juice, and Benedictine to the food processor. Press the pulse and blend until smooth. Stir in grenadine syrup and serve.

If you liked Japanese recipes, discover to how cook DELICIOUS recipes from **Balkan** countries!

Within these pages, you'll learn 35 authentic recipes from a Balkan cook. These aren't ordinary recipes you'd find on the Internet, but recipes that were closely guarded by our Balkan mothers and passed down from generation to generation.

Main Dishes, Appetizers, and Desserts included!

If you want to learn how to make Croatian green peas stew, and 32 other authentic Balkan recipes, then start with our book!

Order at www.balkanfood.org/cook-books/ for only $2,99

If you're a **Mediterranean** dieter who wants to know the secrets of the Mediterranean diet, dieting, and cooking, then you're about to discover how to master cooking meals on a Mediterranean diet right now!

In fact, if you want to know how to make Mediterranean food, then this new e-book - "The 30-minute Mediterranean diet" - gives you the answers to many important questions and challenges every Mediterranean dieter faces, including:

- How can I succeed with a Mediterranean diet?
- What kind of recipes can I make?
- What are the key principles to this type of diet?
- What are the suggested weekly menus for this diet?
- Are there any cheat items I can make?

... and more!

If you're serious about cooking meals on a Mediterranean diet and you really want to know how to make Mediterranean food, then you need to grab a copy of "The 30-minute Mediterranean diet" right now.

Prepare **111 recipes with several ingredients in less than 30 minutes**!

Order at www.balkanfood.org/cook-books/ for only $2,99

What could be better than a home-cooked meal? Maybe only a **Greek** homemade meal.

Do not get discouraged if you have no Greek roots or friends. Now you can make a Greek food feast in your kitchen.

This ultimate Greek cookbook offers you 111 best dishes of this cuisine! From more famous gyros to more exotic *Kota Kapama* this cookbook keeps it easy and affordable.

All the ingredients necessary are wholesome and widely accessible. The author's picks are as flavorful as they are healthy. The dishes described in this cookbook are "what Greek mothers have made for decades."

Full of well-balanced and nutritious meals, this handy cookbook includes many vegan options. Discover a plethora of benefits of Mediterranean cuisine, and you may fall in love with cooking at home.

Inspired by a real food lover, this collection of delicious recipes will taste buds utterly satisfied.

Order at www.balkanfood.org/cook-books/ for only $2,99

Maybe to try exotic **Syrian** cuisine?

From succulent *sarma*, soups, warm and cold salads to delectable desserts, the plethora of flavors will satisfy the most jaded foodie. Have a taste of a new culture with this **traditional Syrian cookbook**.

Order at www.balkanfood.org/cook-books/ for only $2,99

Maybe **Polish** or **Korean** cuisine?

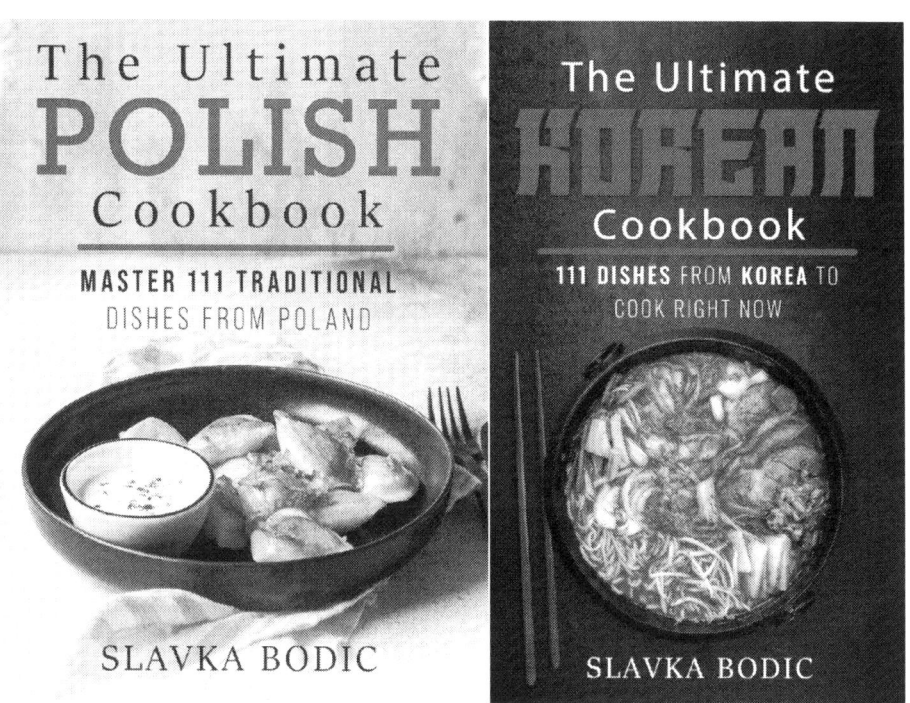

Order at www.balkanfood.org/cook-books/ for only $2,99

Or **Peruvian**?

Order at www.balkanfood.org/cook-books/ for only $2,99

ONE LAST THING

If you enjoyed this book or found it useful, I'd be very grateful if you could find the time to post a short review on Amazon. Your support really does make a difference and I read all the reviews personally, so I can get your feedback and make this book even better.

Thanks again for your support!

Please send me your feedback at

www.balkanfood.org

Printed in Great Britain
by Amazon